CAMBRIDGE CLASSICAL STUDIES

General Editors

D. L. PAGE, W. K. C. GUTHRIE, A. H. M. JONES

TOWARDS A
TEXT OF CICERO
'AD ATTICUM'

TRANSACTIONS OF THE
CAMBRIDGE PHILOLOGICAL SOCIETY
VOLUME X, 1959

TRANSACTIONS OF THE
CAMBRIDGE PHILOLOGICAL SOCIETY

(NEW SERIES)

VOLUME VII (1937), R. E. Witt, *Albinus*

VOLUME VIII (1953), G. P. Shipp, *Studies in the Language of Homer.*

VOLUME IX (1956), D. R. Shackleton Bailey, *Propertiana.*

Volumes II–VI of the earlier series of *Transactions* are available in parts: for details and prices apply to the Hon. Secretary of the Cambridge Philological Society, Peterhouse, Cambridge.

TOWARDS A TEXT OF CICERO 'AD ATTICUM'

BY

D. R. SHACKLETON BAILEY
LITT.D., F.B.A.

Fellow of Jesus College, Cambridge
University Lecturer in Tibetan

CAMBRIDGE
AT THE UNIVERSITY PRESS
1960

PUBLISHED BY

THE SYNDICS OF THE CAMBRIDGE UNIVERSITY PRESS

Bentley House, 200 Euston Road, London, N.W. 1
American Branch: 32 East 57th Street, New York 22, N.Y.

©

CAMBRIDGE UNIVERSITY PRESS

1960

60-315

Printed in Great Britain at the University Press, Cambridge
(Brooke Crutchley, University Printer)

CONTENTS

PREFACE

It is well known that C. A. Lehmann's reappraisal of the MSS. of these Letters, carried into effect by H. Sjögren up to the end of Book XII, produced a bigger and better apparatus criticus than any previously possible. Its importance for Cicero's text has often been overestimated, but it is not too much to say that a modern editor stands far closer to the archetype than his predecessors. Many minor corruptions have disappeared from the vulgate in consequence; but since the archetype was itself deeply corrupt, and since Sjögren, whose influence is still dominant, was no critic, the gain has been mingled. Modern texts certainly contain less that Cicero did not write than Wesenberg's or Müller's; no less certainly they contain more that Cicero could not possibly have written. Only when adequate critical judgment has been applied to what Lehmann and Sjögren have given us shall we have a critical edition worth the name.

These notes are intended as a contribution to such an edition and as a preliminary to a new Oxford Classical Text of Books IX–XVI which I have myself undertaken. It should go without saying that they neither are nor pretend to be comprehensive or final. As for comprehensiveness, I have published other such notes elsewhere[1] and may publish more. As for finality, part of my purpose is to elicit criticisms which may modify my conclusions before they are incorporated in my text. Originally I had intended a series of articles, and the choice of book form has been prompted simply by convenience and the benevolent initiative of the Council of the Cambridge Philological Society.

Such apparatus criticus as I have provided (I often ignore variants which do not affect the points at issue) is derived almost entirely from printed sources, chiefly Sjögren, except that in Books XIII–XVI I have made some use of my own collations of *b* and *m*. The only modern apparatus for these books is Moricca's (1953), which is unreliable and incomplete—*b* and *m* are tacitly ignored. However,

---

[1] *Proc. Camb. Phil. Soc.* III (1954–5), pp. 26–31, ibid. IV (1956–7), pp. 13–18, *J.R.S.* 1956, pp. 57–64.

I have gone far enough with the task of collation to know that, as was to be expected, it is of little moment for critical purposes.

I have to acknowledge financial assistance from the Cambridge Philological Society and the Faculty Board of Classics. My chief personal obligation is to Professor W. S. Watt, who commented in detail upon an early draft of these notes, with special attention to Books I–X. His unrivalled knowledge of the criticism of the Letters has saved me from many bibliographical errors and omissions. On matters of opinion his help has been still more valuable, leading me to modify many notes and to suppress some. He must not be supposed to agree with all that remains. I am also indebted to Miss M. I. Hubbard, Fellow of St Anne's College, for help in proof-reading. It is a pleasure to acknowledge again the helpfulness and efficiency of the Cambridge University Press.   D. R. S. B.

CAMBRIDGE 1959

SIGLA CODICUM

E   Ambrosianus *E* 14 inf.
G   Parisinus 'Nouv. Fonds' 16248.
H   Landianus 8.
N   Laurentianus ex Conv. Suppr. 49.
O   Taurinensis Lat. 495.
P   Parisinus Lat. 8536.
R   Parisinus Lat. 8538.
V   Palatinus Lat. 1510.
Σ   consensus codicum *EGHNOPRV*, ut quoque loco praesto sunt, aut omnium aut plurimorum.

M   Mediceus 49. 18.
b   Berolinensis ex bibl. Hamiltoniana 168.
d   Laurentianus ex bibl. aedilium 217.
m   Berolinensis ex bibl. Hamiltoniana 166.
s   Urbinas 322.
Δ   consensus codicum *Mbdms*, aut omnium aut plurimorum.

Ω   consensus codicum *Σ* et *Δ*.

C   lectiones margini editionis Cratandrinae adscriptae.
W   fragmenta codicis Wurceburgensis.
Z^b codex Tornesianus a Bosio in commentario citatus.
$Z^β$ codicis Tornesiani lectiones a Bosio codici Parisino 8538 A adscriptae et ab A. C. Clark in *Philol.* 1901, pp. 195 sqq. editae.
Z^l codex Tornesianus teste Lambino.
Z^t codex Tornesianus teste Turnebo.

E^2, G^2 etc. codicum *E*, *b*, etc. correctores. De codicis *M* variis manibus (M^2, M^3, M^4) vide quae scripsit W. S. Watt in praefatione ad editionem Epistularum ad Quintum Fratrem, pp. 3–4.

BOOK I

1. 1. 1   competitores, qui certi esse videantur, Galba et Antonius et
Q. Cornificius. puto te in hoc aut risisse aut ingemuisse. ut
frontem ferias, sunt qui etiam Caesonium *putent*. *Aquilium* non
arbitrabamur, qui denegavit et iuravit morbum et illud suum
regnum iudiciale opposuit.

putent. Aquilium *vulg.*, putent iaquillum *G*, putent et Aquillum *H*, putent nam
qui illum *N*, putant (-ent *P*) qui illum *VO¹RP*, potentia qui illum *Δ*

The discrepancies in the MSS. are not necessarily significant, but
if anything ought to stand between *putent* and *Aquilium* I think it is
iam (*iā*) rather than the praenomen *C.* (Constans).[1] *iam* for *deinde* is
common in Cicero and elsewhere: see *T.L.L.* VII, 121 ff.   *nam*
(elliptical: 'I don't mention Aquilius, for...') is also possible.

1. 2. 1   abs te *etiam* diu nihil litterarum

The choice between *tam diu* (edd. vett.) and *iam diu* (Boot) is
variously made. There is nothing to support the former comparable
to 6. 9. 1 *quas [litteras] quidem cum exspectassem iam diu, Fam.*
7. 9. 1 *iam diu ignoro quid agas; nihil enim scribis*, ibid. 7. 13. 1 *ob
eamque causam me arbitrarere litteras ad te iam diu non misisse*, ibid.
2. 14 *nam iam diu...nihil novi ad nos adferebatur*.

1. 11. 1   neque epistulae tuae neque nostra legatio

allegatio *s*¹

'*adlegatio* is private; *legatio* public' (TP, i.e. Tyrrell and Purser,
following Malaespina). Hence *adlegatio* has long been the vulgate.
I am sceptical. On the one hand *adlegatio* comes only twice elsewhere in classical Latin, *Verr.* 2. 1. 44 and 136, though *adlegare* is
more frequent. On the other, *legare* and *legatus* are certainly used of
private missions: 14. 19. 4 *huc enim Caerellia missa ab istis est legata*
(*allegata* Lambinus) *ad me*, Cat. 66. 57 *ipsa suum Zephyritis eo
famulum legarat*, Ov. *Ex P.* 2. 2. 43 *mandatique mei legatus suscipe
causam*, Petr. 107. 9 *si gratiam a legato moliebantur*. The change is
very slight, but is it worth making?

[1] Followed by Moricca. I give this information only here.

1

1. 13. 3   Messalla vehementer adhuc agit severe

Clark[1] was not the first to add *et* after *agit*; Lambinus was before him. Considering not only 16. 15. 2 *agi prorsus vehementer et severe volo* but also *Verr.* 2. 5. 133 *esse severe ac vehementer vindicatum*, *Catil.* 4. 12 *me severum vehementemque praebebo*, and Gell. 10. 19. 1 *severa atque vehementi obiurgatione*, I should follow them.

1. 14. 2   locutus ita est in senatu ut omnia illius ordinis consulta γενικῶς laudaret, mihique, ut adsedit, dixit se putare satis ab se *etiam* de istis rebus esse responsum.

de istis] demptis *C*, de istis ipsis *N*

de istis rebus is usually understood as Pompey's own words, 'those exploits of yours'. Like Reid[2] I find this hard to square with the context, and I also doubt whether Atticus could reasonably be expected to understand it without the assistance of quotation marks. Would not Cicero have written *de nostris*, or *de meis*, or *de meis ipsius*—all early conjectures? An even more damaging and to my mind conclusive objection is the awkwardness of *etiam*. Can one imagine a speaker remarking to his neighbour as he sits down 'I think I have said enough about your affairs *also*'? I suggest *iam*, taking *de istis rebus* to mean the matter under debate. Pompey had already been forced to deliver himself about the Bona Dea affair in a *contio* (§ 1); now he had done so in the senate. He hoped that would suffice.

1. 16. 8   Clodium praesentem fregi in senatu cum oratione perpetua plenissima gravitatis tum altercatione *eiusmodi*; ex qua licet pauca degustes *et sqq.*

eiusmodi *M*[3] (*sed del.*) *mΣGH*: huiusmodi *MbdsN*

According to what is now the generally accepted valuation of the MSS. *eiusmodi* has the better authority. Most modern editors choose *huiusmodi*, presumably because they think it better Latin in the sense required ('of the following kind'). That is not so: cf. 14. 2. 3 *id eiusmodi est*, Rosc. Am. 17 *homines eiusmodi: alter...gladiator habetur* et sqq., *Verr.* 2. 2. 31 *si iudicium sit eiusmodi*, Clu. 179, Pro

[1] *C.R.* 1900, p. 178.   [2] *Hermath.* XIII (1905), p. 100.

Cornelio ap. Ascon. 60, *Mur.* 61, *Font.* 29, *Fin.* 4. 14 (Madvig's note inadequate), Val. Max. 9. 3. 4, Sen. *Ben.* 6. 11. 1, *N.Q.* 1. 1. 7, 1. 3. 2, *Ep.* 81. 16, Col. 8. 5. 11, Cels. 6. 6. 6, Petr. 100. 3, Gell. 2. 6. 9, 11. 3. 1. In *Ad Her.* 1. 24 the MSS. vary.

1. 16. 10   surgit pulchellus puer, obicit mihi me ad Baias fuisse. falsum, sed tamen quid huic? 'simile est', inquam, 'quasi in operto dicas fuisse.'

huic] hoc *C*

So modern editors, except that most read *hoc* for *huic*, and that Sjögren and others begin the *oratio recta* at *falsum*. But *quid hoc?* is not Latin for 'what of that?', and 'what business is that of his?' would be *quid ad hunc?* Repunctuation is needed: *falsum, sed tamen* —'*quid? hoc simile est*', inquam, '*quasi in operto dicas fuisse?*' 'A falsehood, but never mind that. "Well," say I, "is that like saying I was in a private place?"' For the aposiopesis cf. *Fam.* 2. 16. 10 *velim ita sit. sed tamen*—, *Att.* 12. 17 *quamquam quid ad me? verum tamen*— et sim.[1] For *quid* and the position of *inquam* cf. *Quinct.* 78 *ut...quemvis commoveret (etenim...accedat), verum tamen:* '*quid? si*', inquit, '*habes eiusmodi causam*' et sqq., *De Or.* 1. 10. 2 '*quid? mihi vos nunc*', inquit Crassus, '*tamquam alicui Graeculo...quaestiunculam...ponitis?*', Gell. 13. 25. 24 '*quip igitur? simile est*', inquit, '*apud eundem in* "*praeda*" *et* "*manubiis?*"', Apul. *Met.* 1. 15 '*quid? tu*', inquit, *ignoras latronibus infestari vias?*'

Tenney Frank[2] argues from the parallel fragment (4. 2) of *Or. in Clod. et Cur.* that Cicero by his own admission *was* at Baiae and that *falsum* should therefore be changed to *salsum* (Manutius). But no wit is apparent in Clodius' taunt, and the fragment makes it clear that Cicero was on his estate (*in suis praediis*) in the neighbourhood of Baiae, no doubt the Pompeianum. This was close enough to Baiae to allow of Clodius' charge, and in the speech Cicero evidently did not trouble to point out the literal inaccuracy.[3]

in operto with reference to the rites of the Bona Dea comes in Ascon. 43 (adduced by Corradus) as well as in *Parad.* 32; of other secret rites in Liv. 39. 14. 9, Col. 3. 10. 10, Apul. *Met.* 9. 9.

[1] *sed tamen* could also be taken resumptively as in 7. 1. 9 *hoc primum, quod accessit cura dolori meo, sed tamen hoc, quicquid est, Precianum* et sqq.

[2] *Amer. J. Phil.* 1920, pp. 277 f.

[3] Cf. TP on 2. 8. 2 (vol. 1, p. 293).

1. 16. 13   Lurco autem tr. pl., qui *magistratum simul* cum lege Aelia
iniit, solutus est et Aelia et Fufia *et sqq.*

simul] insimul *Mm*

There are plenty of conjectures, but the best in my opinion is
ignored save for a bare mention in TP.[1] That is Clark's:[2] *qui
magistratus simultatem cum lege Aelia iniit.* For the sense see TP's
addenda, vol. I, note II. For the wording cf. Liv. 1. 59. 7 *tribunum
celerum, in quo tum magistratu forte Brutus erat,* 30. 7. 5 *sufetes, quod
velut consulare imperium apud eas erat,* 38. 30. 4 *damiurgis civitatium,
qui summus est magistratus,* Just. 18. 4. 5 *sacerdoti Herculis, qui honos
secundus a rege erat.* The personifications need not alarm: *Leg. Agr.*
2. 14 *bellum nescio quod habet susceptum consulatus cum tribunatu,* Val.
Max. 2. 9. 8 *iam haec censura ex foro in castra transcendit, quae neque
timeri neque decipi voluit hostem,* Plat. *Crit.* 50–54.

1. 17. 4   de iis litteris quas ad te Thessalonica misit et de sermonibus
quos ab illo et Romae apud amicos tuos et in itinere habitos
putas, ecquid *tantum* causae sit ignoro, sed omnis in tua posita
est humanitate mihi spes huius levandae molestiae.

et quid *Ω, corr. Manutius*

ecquid tantum causae sit ignoro can only mean 'I don't know
whether there is any sufficient reason [or excuse] for Quintus' conduct'. It is not for nothing that translators in their various fashions
boggle at this. For Cicero, here at such obvious pains to be tactful,
would never have suggested that his brother might have had
sufficient grounds for his unfriendly behaviour to Atticus, only that
he might have had *some* grounds. *tandem* (Ernesti) is one possibility,
tamen ('after all') another. But I prefer *tantulum*, 'some trifle of
justification', comparing 4. 8a. 3 *tantulane causa?, Verr.* 2. 2. 93
tantulum morae, Att. 15. 27. 3 *nec quicquam posthac non modo tantum
sed ne tantulum quidem praeterieris.* Diminutives are often so corrupted: cf. 1. 8. 3 *delici⟨ol⟩ae,* 8. 13. 2 *vill⟨ul⟩as,* 9. 15. 6 *pauc⟨ul⟩os,*
10. 11. 2 *lent⟨ul⟩um.*

---

[1] Vol. I, p. 217.

[2] Sternkopf had previously proposed *qui magistratum in simultate cum,* but
later changed his mind (*Wochenschrift f. Klass. Philol.* 1917, pp. 857–9).

1. 19. 9   ex ipso s.c. intellegere potes aliam rem tum relatam, hoc autem de liberis populis *sine causa* additum.

'Manifestum est corrupta esse. . . verba *sine causa* (nam sine causa an cum causa additum hoc fuerit, nihil omnino ad id, de quo Cicero scribit, pertinet).' So Madvig.[1] It is no answer to say with Müller that *sine causa* means 'ohne Zweck', for, apart from the absurdity of this, Servilius' motive or lack of it *is* nothing to the point. What Cicero means is that the clause was irrelevant to the decree, added without external and manifest reason. Scholars do not seem to be well acquainted with this use of *sine causa*, noticed by Cicero himself in *Fat.* 24 *communi igitur consuetudine sermonis abutimur cum ita dicimus, velle aliquid quempiam aut nolle sine causa; ita enim dicimus 'sine causa' ut dicamus sine externa et antecedente causa, non sine aliqua.* He has it in *Verr.* 2. 1. 158 *quos iste annuerat in suum consilium sine causa subsortiebatur* ('without the least justification', Greenwood), 2. 5. 22 *cur. . .sine causa de carcere emitti iusserit, Clu.* 27 *arcessit subito sine causa puerum,* 181 *sine causa in quaestionem postulavit.* It is common enough in other writers. In *Bell. Alex.* 39. 1 *Domitius autem, cum. . .neque se tuto discessurum arbitraretur si condiciones quas reiecerat rursus appeteret aut sine causa discederet,* there is no more occasion for Hofmann's *si negatis* or Du Pontet's obelus than in this passage for Orelli's *s.c.* or Madvig's *in eam causam.*

1. 20. 1   in iis rebus quae mihi asperius a nobis atque nostris et iniucundius actae videbantur

Cicero cannot here be blaming himself for anything in his conduct towards Atticus. He is a peacemaker between Atticus and Quintus, without responsibility for their differences. The best of many conjectures is Corradus' *atque ⟨adeo a⟩ nostris,* to which nobody seems to have paid the smallest attention. *a nobis,* 'on our side', refers to Quintus; but a correction is added to avoid ambiguity. A neighbouring letter, 1. 17. 9, has this purely corrective *atque adeo: ego princeps in adiutoribus atque adeo secundus.* For *nobis* and *nostris* cf. 15. 4. 4 *et maxime quid nostris faciendum sit, quid etiam nobis.*

[1] *Adv.* III, pp. 167f.

BOOK II

2. 1. 5   'non consulare', inquies, 'dictum.' fateor; sed ego illam
odi male consularem. 'ea est enim seditiosa, ea cum viro bellum
gerit', neque solum cum Metello sed etiam cum Fabio, quod
eos *nihil* esse moleste fert.

ego odi illam *VOP*, illam ego odi *s*   ni(c)hil esse *M²ENVRP*, nichil in hoc
esse *m*, nihil *O¹*, esse in hoc esse *M*, mihi esse *M³bdsGH*

All recent editors obelize here except TP, who read *in hoc esse* and
explain after Junius and Boot 'operam dare ne Clodius trib. plebis
fiat'. Read *nihili* and all is plain: 'Clodia wages war not only with
her husband [Metellus] but also with Fabius [her lover] because he
objects to them [Clodia and Clodius] being such good for nothings.'
Fabius objected to Clodia's relations with her brother just referred to
in the unconsular jest.

It is tempting so to translate the text as it stands. But from
Ennius, *Fr. Scen.* 423 (Vahlen) *illic est nugator, nil, non nauci homo*[1]
onwards *nihil esse* with a personal subject implies insignificance or
incompetence rather than moral obliquity: 1. 19. 4 *ille alter nihil ita
est ut plane quid emerit nesciat, Fam.* 7. 33. 1 *nihil sumus* [sc. *in
eloquentia*], *Div. in Caec.* 47 *ipse nihil est, nihil potest, Brut.* 178 *in
causis publicis nihil, in privatis satis veterator videbatur* (in Tib. 1. 5. 30
at iuvet in tota me nihil esse domo it means 'be a cypher', in *Q. Fr.*
1. 2. 14 and Mart. 2. 64. 10 'be as good as dead'). Clodius and
Clodia were by no means *nihil*, but in Cicero's opinion they were
emphatically *nihili*: *Tusc.* 3. 18 *nequitia...ab eo quod nequicquam est
in tali homine, ex quo idem nihili dicitur* (see Dougan–Henry ad loc.;
but they are wrong about *Q. Fr.* 1. 2. 14), Pl. *Asin.* 472 *impure,
nihili*, 859 *madidum, nihili, incontinentem*, et sim.

Malaespina was right to take *male* with *odi*, a sound Ciceronian
colloquialism (*T.L.L.* VIII, 244. 49 ff.). The order, for which cf.
Pl. *Men.* 189 *odi male*, Petr. 56. 2 *si illos odi pessime*, presents no
difficulty. That *male consularem* could represent *consule indignam*
seems to me incredible, despite the preceding *non consulare dictum.*
illam consularem=consularem illam feminam: cf. Suet. *Aug.* 69. 1

---

[1] Vahlen and others read *nihili* (Ursinus).

feminam consularem, Liv. 7. 4. 5 *dictatorius iuvenis. consularem* probably reflects on the airs Clodia gave herself, and is not really parallel to the preceding *consulare*, though Cicero may not quite have appreciated that. Compare the falsely balanced clauses in 3. 17. 3 *quid te aut horter quod facis aut agam gratias quod non exspectas* and the false antithesis of *Leg. Man.* 39 *hiemis enim, non avaritiae perfugium maiores nostri in sociorum atque amicorum tectis esse voluerunt.*

2. 7. 5 Castricianum mendum nos corrigemus, et tamen ad me Quintus HS ccɪɔɔ ɪɔɔ scripserat, non ⟨ut⟩ ad sororem, HS xxx a. Terentia tibi salutem dicit.

a *MmP*, at *M^c bdsGHNO²*, ad *V*, a te *R*

XXX, XXXIII, XXXVI, and *XXXM* have been conjectured. Why not *XXXV*? 35,000 might easily have been confused with 25,000, and *u* mistaken by a copyist for *a*. The first letter of *Terentia* accounts for *at*.

2. 8. 1 bene habemus nos, si in his spes est. opinor, aliud agamus.

But many editors: *bene habemus; nos, si in his spes est, opinor, aliud agamus.* 'There is little to choose between the rival punctuations. *bene habere* is common (of persons) both with and without the personal pronoun after it.'[1] *bene habere* (of persons) without the personal pronoun after (or before) it is so far from common that the only classical example I know is [Quint.] *Decl.* 377 (Ritter, p. 420. 18) *Scipio, inquit, bene habet.*[2] This does not occur in *T.L.L.* vi. 3, 2452. 15 ff., where we do however meet several of *belle habere* and one of *male habere*, Cels. 2. 1. 18. This last may be misplaced, for the passage can be punctuated *propriae etiam dentientium gingivarum exulcerationes...alvi deiectiones, maximeque caninis dentibus orientibus, male habent* [sc. *infantes tenerosque adhuc pueros*].

2. 9. 1 subito cum mihi dixisset Caecilius quaestor puerum se Romam mittere, haec scripsi raptim, ut tuos mirificos cum Publio dialogos, cum eos de quibus scribis, tum illum quem abdis et ais longum esse, quae ad ea responderis, perscribere.

[1] Reid, *Hermath.* xiii (1905), p. 374.
[2] But Liv. *Epit.* 114 *imperator bene se habet.*

In the vulgate *dialogos* is followed by *elicerem* (edd. vett.), doubtless as purely conjectural a supplement as Reid's *exigerem*. Neither
is apposite. Why should Cicero demand what he has already got?
de quibus scribis in contrast with *abdis* shows that Atticus had sent an
account of all but one of the dialogues. Perhaps add *remunerarer*.
But Professor Watt's suggestion 'something like *velim* [instead of
ut] *mihi diligentius perscribas tuos mirificos* etc.' may well be right.

2. 14. 2   et tamen illud probem: 'magnum quid adgrediamur et
multae cogitationis atque otii.' sed tamen satis fiet a nobis
neque parcetur labori.

I have little doubt that *magnum...otii* is a quotation from
Atticus' letter, not 'a former promise of his own' (TP). 'Sed ille
[Atticus] non scripsisset *aggrediamur*' (Boot). Why not? 'Let us
begin' is a friendly way of saying 'begin': cf. 7. 3. 11 '*solvamus*'
inquis, *Fam.* 8. 5. 1 *adsequeremur*, 10. 25. 2 *consecuti sumus*, *Quinct.*
45 *possumus*, *Brut.* 332 *futuri sumus*. For *probem* perhaps read *probe*
with Manutius and a 'codex Maffei' of Malaespina (cf. 14. 8. 1 *de
Mario probe*, 15. 2. 2 *de Menedemo probe*, 15. 21. 2 *quod ad Xenonem*,
probe).

2. 17. 1–2   haec...non deflebimus...sed conferemus tranquillo
animo di immortales neque tam me εὐελπιστία consolatur, ut
antea, quam ἀδιαφορία.

di immortales is very rarely found in Cicero apart from an
exclamation. The few exceptions, *Mur.* 84, *Post. Red. ad Quir.* 4,
Pis. 45 (a rhetorical question), *Phil.* 11. 10, belong to contexts so
highly rhetorical as to prove the rule. *di boni* likewise seems to be
found only in exclamations and questions. Here, therefore, the
solution will lie not in transposition or change of letters but in something like ...*animo*. ⟨*quam enim sum tranquillo*⟩, *di immortales!* Professor Watt suggests *sed conferemus* [cf. 1. 20. 1 fin.]. ⟨*quam sum*⟩
tranquillo animo, di immortales!

2. 22. 5   puto *Pompeium Crasso urgente*, si tu aderis, qui per
βοῶπιν ex ipso intellegere possis, qua fide ab illis agatur, nos
aut sine molestia aut certe sine errore futuros.

I cannot think that Cicero wrote this as it stands; the mention of pressure from Crassus is, as Reid pointed out,[1] too casual, and the relation of the ablative absolute to the rest of the sentence too obscure. *Pompeio Caesarem* (Reid) is palaeographically poor. It looks again as if something has dropped out, e.g. *puto Pompeium Crasso urgente ⟨vacillare, sed⟩ si* et sqq.

2. 24. 2 introductus Vettius primo negabat se umquam cum Curione restitisse

constitisse *C*

I prefer *restitisse* to *constitisse* (despite *T.L.L.* IV, 464. 68–76), and either to *rem constituisse* (Reid). For the first in the sense *mansisse colloquendi causa* there are better parallels than Ter. *Andr.* 344, *Eun.* 337: Phaedr. 3. 7. 3 *dein, salutati invicem* / *ut restiterunt*, Plin. *Paneg.* 48. 3 *remoramur, resistimus ut in communi domo*. But I suspect that Reid's *usquam* is right; cf. Ter. *Andr.* 432 *hic nunc me credit aliquam sibi fallaciam* / *portare et ea me hic restitisse gratia*.

2. 24. 3 quod dixerat adulescentium consilium ut in foro [cum] gladiatoribus Gabini Pompeium adorirentur.

Müller adds *id fuisse* after *dixerat* for a good and obvious cause. It is simpler to add *id* after *quod*.

2. 24. 3 idque ita *actum* esset, nisi Curiones rem ante ad Pompeium detulissent.

The usual alteration to *factum* (Ernesti) is hardly necessitated by the chance occurrence of *id esse actum* in a different sense three lines previously; and there is nothing to be said for Boot's deletion of *ita*. Cf. 11. 9. 2 *nisi res acta sic esset*. Nor can I see the least reason for the vulgate in 7. 7. 7 '*quid ergo*', *inquis*, '⟨*f*⟩*acturus* (Wesenberg) *es?*' Sjögren's observation that M has *factum* for *actum* in *Fam.* 8. 4. 4 and 9. 18. 4 scarcely supports it. True, we find *quid facturus sim* in 7. 7. 5; but *ipse quid sis acturus* in 7. 22. 2 (sim. 5. 18. 4, 7. 13 a. 3, 7. 16. 2, 8. 14. 3, 9. 1. 2; cf. 8. 3. 1, 8. 9. 2, 12. 2. 2) and *sed quid es acturus?* in Pl. *Pseud.* 751 (cf. ibid. 395, *Capt.* 789, *Pers.* 400, Sen. *Contr.* 1. 1. 1, Curt. 10. 2. 14, Plin. *Ep.* 9. 32).

[1] *Hermath.* XIII (1905), p. 391.

2. 24. 4   quod si impetrasset, iudicia fore videbantur. ea nos, utpote
qui nihil contemnere solemus, non pertimescebamus.

solebamus *V*

Subsequent editors[1] read with Wesenberg ⟨*non contemnebamus
sed*⟩ *non pertimescebamus*. Tyrrell, who has a note on the point in his
edition of the *Miles*, might have remembered that Plautus uses
utpote qui to introduce something which modifies or detracts from
the main statement, as well as something which accounts for it: *Mil.*
528 *similiorem mulierem | magi'que eandem, ut pote quae non sit
eadem, non reor | deos facere posse, Rud.* 462 *sati' nequam sum, utpote
qui hodie amare inceperim* (just so *fortis ut Iudaeus* can mean 'brave
for a Jew' as well as 'brave as a Jew should be'). There is no reason
to deny the same usage to Cicero, whose only other example of
utpote qui is in *Phil.* 5. 30. Translate 'for a man who isn't prone to
despise any danger'.

soleamus (Orelli) or *soleremus* (R. Klotz)? This calls for more
research, but my instinct is for the former, since an epistolary tense
does not suit a habit.

ibid.   modo caedem timueramus, quem ⟨metum⟩ oratio fortissimi
senis, Q. Consi⟨di⟩, discusserat. *eam* quam cotidie timere
poteramus subito exorta est. quid quaeris? nihil me fortunatius
est Catulo cum splendore vitae tum mortis tempore.

quem metum *Madvig*: qu(a)e *ΔO*², quam *Σ*   eam quam *codd. plerique*, ea
inquam *Mm*, eam inquam quam *P*, ea quam *sH*   mortis *Lambinus*: hoc *Ω*

The second sentence has not been satisfactorily emended after
many attempts. I doubt if any change is needed beyond the palaeographically trifling one of *eam* (*eā*) to *causa* (*cā*). Recently, says
Cicero, he and his party had been afraid of a massacre by the
triumvirs, but Considius' boldness had temporarily dispelled
anxiety; suddenly a pretext for such a massacre [the Vettius inci-
dent], such as might continually have been feared, had cropped up.
caedis can the more easily be understood from *caedem* because the
expression *causa caedis* is a familiar one: *Fam.* 12. 25. 4 *meque tum
elicere vellet ad caedis causam, Dom.* 115 *meus discessus isti causam
caedis eripuit, Phil.* 3. 30 *caedis et incendiorum causam quaesierit,*

---

[1] Except Boot, who obelizes, and Winstedt, who mistranslates.

Liv. 3. 36. 5 *ratis caedis causam ac principium quaeri*, Tac. *Hist.* 2. 52
causam et initium caedis quaerebant, 4. 1 *initium id perfringendarum
domuum, vel si resisteretur, causa caedis* (otherwise in *Agric.* 7. 2,
'motive for murder'). Possibly *iam*, to contrast with *modo*, should be
added before *causa*, but I think this hardly necessary.

In the next sentence editors read with Lambinus *nihil me ⟨in-
fortunatius, nihil⟩ fortunatius Catulo*. It matters comparatively little
that dictionaries record no other example of *infortunatus* between
Terence and Apuleius, nor of *infortunatior* at any period. Cicero
may have been an egoist, but he was not a fool; and it is mere
fatuity for a man whose party is threatened with massacre to write
that *he* is therefore the most unfortunate thing on earth. In reality
Cicero's mind here is plainly *not* on himself, though it turns that
way in the next sentence, *nos tamen* et sqq. Something, of course,
has disappeared after *me*. Perhaps *hercule*, since *me iudice* for *meo
iudicio* seems to be un-Ciceronian.

BOOK III

3. 7. 3   quem quidem ego nec ⟨quo⟩modo visurus nec ut dimissurus
            sim scio

quomodo *edd. vett.*: modo *MmΣ*, indo (?) *d*, ubi *b*, abmodo *s*, ubi modo *M*ᶜ
ut *Bosius*: vi *N*, cui *E*, vidi *GH*, ubi *ΔVO²*, *om. P*

   quomodo satisfies all requirements.[1] Was it the variation *quomodo
. . .ut* which made Constans prefer *quem quidem ego nec modo ⟨ut⟩
visurus nec ut dimissurus sim scio*? Cf. *Rep.* 2. 43 *quamvis. . .ut*, *Phil.*
5. 14 *quemadmodum. . .quomodo*, Tac. *Hist.* 3. 77 *nec virtutibus, ut
boni, sed, quomodo pessimus quisque, vitiis valebat.* Monosyllables
constantly fall out of MSS., as *quo* itself has done from two in 4. 6. 2.

3. 10. 1 (17 June 58)   nam si erit causa, si quid agetur, si spem
            videro, aut ibidem opperiar aut me ad te conferam; sin, ut tu
            scribis, ista evanuerint, aliud aliquid videbimus.

   'Atticus did *not* write him reassuring letters', TP, on the strength
of 3. 14. 1, where the text is uncertain, and 3. 13. 1, which makes if

[1] Cf. Lehmann, *De Cic. ad Att. ep.* pp. 140 ff.

anything the other way. In reality the correspondence abounds in proofs that around this date Atticus had at any rate tried to sound hopeful. April 29 (3. 7. 3): *de re publica video te colligere omnia quae putes aliquam spem mihi posse adferre mutandarum rerum.* June 13 (3. 9. 2): Cicero says he is sustained and comforted by Atticus' letter, though he could see between the lines that his friend was not really hopeful. June 27 (3. 11. 1): Cicero is stopping at Thessalonica because of Atticus' letters and *quidam boni nuntii.* July 17 (3. 12. 1): *tu quidem sedulo argumentaris quid sit sperandum...spem ostendis secundum comitia.* August 5 (3. 13. 1): Atticus, having nothing cheerful to write, had not written. August, first half (*Q. Fr.* 1. 4. 2): Cicero had stayed in Thessalonica on the strength of hopeful reports from Atticus and others. August 17 (3. 15. 6): Atticus has been hiding unpalatable news. August 19 (3. 16): a plea for greater frankness. The more Cicero studies his friend's letters the plainer it appears that though hopeful in tone they contain no solid ground for encouragement. Perhaps in response to this appeal, Atticus does now seem to have written in a less optimistic vein. September 4 (3. 17. 2): *cetera quae ad me eisdem litteris scribis de nostra spe intellego esse languidiora quam alii ostendunt.* Mid September (3. 18. 2): *tuae autem litterae sunt variae; neque enim me desperare vis nec temere sperare.* September 15 (3. 19. 2): *me tuae litterae numquam in tantam spem adduxerunt quantam aliorum. ac tamen mea spes etiam tenvior semper fuit quam tuae litterae,* i.e. Atticus had been less encouraging than, for example, Quintus, who *omnia mittit spei plena* (3. 18. 2).

As for 3. 14. 1 Cicero assuredly never wrote *etsi scio te me iis epistulis potius et meas spes solitum esse remorari.* What he did write I do not know.

To return to 3. 10. 1, it should now be clear that translations like 'si en revanche, comme tu me l'écris, ces chances-là doivent s'évanouir' are ruled out by the facts of the case. And, even if they were not, how then could Cicero continue thus: 'So far, to be sure,[1] you give me no sign[2] except this disagreement among your friends

---

[1] That is what *omnino* means, not 'absolument rien d'autre'. Incidentally, *si erit causa* in the previous sentence means, not 's'il y a lieu', but 'if there is going to be a cause to fight for', i.e. 'if my case is not just abandoned': cf. 8. 3. 4 *denique nulla causa, nullae vires.*   [2] I.e. no hopeful sign.

(the triumvirs), and that is on any subject rather than on me; so I don't see what good it does me. However, so long as you all (*vos*) want me to hope, I shall obey you'? The argument that division among the triumvirs gave no solid ground for hope implies that Atticus thought, or professed to think, that it did; and Atticus is included in *vos me sperare vultis*.

Are we then to accept the transposition (an old one, known to Corradus) *me ad te conferam, ut tu scribis*? It is tempting, but unnecessary. As Manutius pointed out, Atticus may have written something like *si haec evanuerint, alia videbimus* without expressing the opinion that hopes would indeed be liars: cf. 7. 26. 3 *nisi qui, ut tu scribis, Parthicus casus exstiterit.*

3. 12. 2   sed...quia scripta mihi videtur [*sc.* oratio] neglegentius quam ceterae, puto ex se probari non esse meam.

  ex se *M³bdsEGHV*, esse *MmO*, posse *M⁴* (*in marg.*) *NRP*

'In structura *ex se probari* ne quis haereat, cfr similes has: de Fin. II. 26⁸³ *quae faciat amicitiam...ex se et propter se expetendam*, de N.D. II. 12³², III. 14³⁶.'¹ Add Caes. *B.G.* 5. 27. 4 *id se facile ex humilitate sua probare posse*. It is not the construction that is difficult, but the sense. That could only be 'I think that it is being successfully passed off as not mine by its own character': cf. *Verr.* 2. 5. 78 *in eius locum quem pro illo probare velles*, *Rab. Post.* 41 *vel, si meminerit, oblitum esse facile possit probare*, *Mil.* 65 *mirabar...vulnus in latere, quod acu punctum videretur, pro ictu gladiatoris probari*, *Ad Brut.* 2. 5. 4 *hoc cogere volebat, falsas litteras esse, et, si quaeris, probabat*. What Cicero means is clearly 'I think it can be passed off'. *posse* is indispensable, but it need not obliterate *ex se*. Read *ex se* ⟨*posse*⟩ *probari*.

3. 17. 1   is omnino mentionem nullam factam esse nuntiavit, sed fuisse tamen sermonem de C. Clodi filio.

The topic is a possible accusation of Quintus, who had just returned from the governorship of Asia. It is customary to render 'He reported that absolutely no notice whatever had been given of a prosecution', and to explain *mentionem factam esse* as 'formula foren-

   ¹ Sjögren, *Comm. Tull.* p. 34.

sis quae usurpatur de nomine apud praetorem deferendo'. This is moonshine. In *Quinct.* 37, adduced by Boot, *mentionem fecisse* means simply 'mentioned'. But if the words have their ordinary sense, the second statement contradicts the first. Probably something has fallen out, e.g. *mentionem ⟨P.⟩ nullam*, 'no mention of P. Clodius' as a possible prosecutor.

As in 3. 10. 1, *omnino* ought not to be taken with *nullam*, but as μέν, answered by *sed tamen*. Many Ciceronian commentators have written notes on this concessive use of *omnino*,[1] which translators regularly misunderstand, but neither they nor dictionaries appreciate its frequency.[2] In upwards of sixty examples from Cicero an adversative particle follows, usually *sed* or *sed tamen*, but also *tamen* (*Off.* 1. 79; cf. *Att.* 16. 16c. 12), *ac tamen* (*Sest.* 115, *Att.* 4. 18. 1), *verum tamen* (*Att.* 13. 2a. 2), *verum* (*Off.* 1. 133), *autem* (*Caec.* 64, *Amic.* 98, *Att.* 7. 9. 3), *sin* (*Att.* 6. 3. 9). Occasionally the answering sentence is asyndetic: *Phil.* 11. 7 *maioris omnino est consilii providere ne quid tale accidat, animi non minoris fortiter ferre si evenerit, Amic.* 69 *egregium virum omnino, sibi nequaquam parem.* Frequently there is no answering sentence, and *omnino* ('no doubt', 'to be sure') implies a modification of what precedes: e.g. 6. 2. 7 *audio omnino Scaptium paenitere.* Except for a few examples in the younger Pliny (1. 17. 2, 2. 4. 3, 2. 19. 6, 5. 9. 7, 6. 15. 3) this use is scarcely found in other writers. I can cite only Varro, *L.L.* 9. 106.

3. 24. 2   tota res quo *loco* sit velim ad me scribas

Does Cicero elsewhere write *quo loco* when he means 'in what state', as Horace (*Ep.* 1. 12. 25) and Virgil (*Aen.* 2. 322) do? I think not. He does write *quo loci*: 7. 16. 3 *quo loci sit res*, 8. 10 *respondit se quod in nummis haberet nescire quo loci esset*, 1. 13. 5 *res eodem est loci quo reliquisti*.

---

[1] Professor Watt refers to Nägelsbach–Müller, ed. 9, pp. 778 f.
[2] Not even Du Mesnil on *Flacc.* 71, who gives eighteen instances from Cicero.

BOOK IV

4. 1. 7 qui si sustulerint religionem, aream praeclaram habebimus; superficiem consules ex senatus consulto aestimabunt; sin aliter, demolientur, suo nomine locabunt, rem totam aestimabunt.

demolientur is understood as referring to Clodius' temple. But, as TP remark, the temple would hardly be pulled down if the consecration were held valid. And if the temple was to come down whether the consecration was invalidated or not, why say *demolientur* only in the second alternative? *locabunt*, too, is intolerably obscure. I agree with Boot that something has been lost, something like *demolientur* ⟨*tamen porticum illam, Catuli restituendam*⟩ *suo nomine locabunt*. Compare what actually happened, 4. 2. 5: *deinde consules porticum Catuli restituendam locarunt; illam porticum redemptores statim sunt demoliti libentissimis omnibus. nobis superficiem aedium consules de consilii sententia aestimarunt HS vicies.*

If the consecration is nullified, Cicero will have the site on which to rebuild and receive compensation for his demolished house. He does not say, and perhaps at this stage does not know, whether the temple and portico will be removed by the consuls, under a state contract, or by himself. If, on the other hand, the consecration is upheld, he will be paid compensation for both site and building. The site will then be public property and no further concern of his. The temple will stay, and only the portico be pulled down and replaced at the public expense.

4. 3. 2 ille *vehemens* ruere, post hunc vero furorem nihil nisi caedem inimicorum cogitare, vicatim ambire, servis aperte spem libertatis ostendere.

vehementer bd   vero om. Δ

demens (Pius: cf. *Phil.* 3. 31 *nec ruere demens nec furere desinit, Dom.* 3 *ille demens* [sc. *Clodius*]) is not the whole answer. *post hunc vero furorem* needs for balance a reference to the past (cf. in the following sentence *etenim antea* followed by *post has ruinas*), otherwise *vero* has no function. Perhaps *ille ve*⟨*l ante*⟩ *demens*.

Later in the paragraph there is mention of a henchman of Clodius, *Decimum designatorem*,[1] known otherwise only from *Dom.* 50 *Decimis et Clodiis auctoribus*.[2] The name is highly suspicious. Decimus as a cognomen does not seem to occur until the third century A.D. When Cicero refers to a man by his praenomen alone, unless this is a rare and distinctive one like Appius, Servius, Faustus, he does it to betoken familiarity (often ironical) or to distinguish him from another person of the same nomen and cognomen; as in 15. 10 and 15. 11. 2 D. Brutus is called Decimus to distinguish him from M. Brutus. Orelli's neglected *Decimium* may be right, though the only contemporary Decimius of whom there is record, C. Decimius of 4. 16. 9, is certainly not the same man. Reading *Decium* and *Deciis* one might suggest identity with the supporter of Antony who is mocked in *Phil.* 11. 13 and 13. 27.

4. 3. 4   Metellus cum prima luce furtim in campum itineribus prope deviis currebat.

How 'almost' a detour? A route is devious, as in 14. 10. 1 *ut Trebonius itineribus deviis proficisceretur in provinciam* and elsewhere, or it is straight. I suggest *properans*. The loss of the last four letters would be nothing extraordinary; e.g. *adhibendus* is reduced to *ad idem* in 10. 14. 3, *ad Terentiam* to *ad te rem* in 1. 12. 1, *quaero* to *quae* in 3. 15. 4, *culpa* to *cui* in 11. 2. 2, *perge* to *per* in 11. 7. 4.

4. 5. 3   The penultimate sentence makes sense in no edition. I would punctuate thus:

> viaticum Crassipes praeripit. tu 'de via recta in hortos?' videtur commodius. ad te postridie scilicet. quid enim tua? sed viderimus.

This must be taken with 4. 12: *Kalendis cogito in hortis Crassipedis quasi in deversorio cenare...inde domum cenatus.* Constans' tentative suggestion that 4. 5 should come between 4. 8 and 4. 12 may well be right.

It is to be assumed that Atticus already knew of Cicero's intention to dine on the night of his return to Rome with his future son-

---

[1] Better *dissignatorem*: see *T.L.L.* s.vv.
[2] Missing apparently in *RE*.

in-law in the suburbs. Atticus is supposed to make a facetious protest. A paterfamilias ought to go straight to his house and family, not to a dinner party *in hortis*. That these were associated with fast living emerges clearly from *Cael.* 27 *eum qui nullum convivium renuerit, qui in hortis fuerit, qui unguenta sumpserit, qui Baias viderit.* Cicero answers that it seems more convenient to do as he proposes (imaginary question, asyndetic answer as, for example, in 4. 8 a. 3 *dices 'tantulane causa?' permulta ad me detulerat non dubia de Firmanis fratribus*). He will visit Atticus the following day; a few hours sooner or later will not make any odds to him (cf. Pl. *Amph.* 1003 *quid id mea?*). But this can be settled later. In fact, the plans are revised in 4. 12.

4. 6. 2   ecce quartae fulmen! sed ille, ut scripsi, non miser, nos vero
 ferrei.

 ferrei *M^cs*: ferei *m*, ferri *MbdNORP*

Editors print *ferrei*, but not all believe in it. *servi, miseri, miserrimi* have been conjectured, and I know good scholars who are convinced that *ferrei* is wrong. I feel sure that it is right.

'Lentulus is not to be pitied; but we (who go on living) are iron of heart'—'nimis patientes, ἀπαθεῖς, qui adhuc vivamus nec voluntaria morte nos (a servitute) liberemus' (Orelli). That is how the words must be taken: not 'but we who are so callous as to live on' (Shuckburgh, supplying *miseri sumus*), much less 'c'est nous qui le sommes, qui avons une santé de fer' (Constans). Kayser's notion that *ferrei* alludes to Hesiod's Iron Age belongs in limbo. Its function is to provide the most forcible of contrasts to *non miser*. The living are not merely unhappy, or even most unhappy, but so unhappy that it is a wonder they can bear to live at all.

If Cicero had written *nos vero ferrei qui vivamus* I imagine few would have complained. *ferreus*, a favourite word with him, is a *mot juste* in this context, as Shuckburgh went some way to show by citing *Amic.* 87 *quis tam esset ferreus qui eam vitam ferre posset?* It is possible there to detect a play on *ferreus* and *ferre*, though I do not credit it. But for an even closer parallel go to Ov. *Met.* 13. 516, where Hecuba over Polyxena's carcass asks *quo ferrea resto?* Similarly *crudelis* ibid. 11. 700: *crudelior ipso | sit mihi mens pelago, si vitam ducere nitar | longius, durus* in [Tib.] 3. 2. 3 *durus et ille fuit, qui tantum ferre dolorem, | vivere et erepta coniuge qui potuit,* and *sceleratus* in *Cons. Liv.* 135. The question is, then, whether *qui vivamus* could fairly be left to the reader's imagination. Surely it could. Cicero has just been deploring his miserable situation. After that, the contrast between Lentulus, lucky to be dead, and *nos*, the living, is enough. Atticus would need no plainer pointer. Add that the misery and dishonour of surviving the downfall of the republic is a commonplace in the Letters: 7. 23. 2 *manebo igitur, etsi vivere* (aposiopesis), 9. 12. 3 *populi Romani exercitus Cn. Pompeium circumsedet. . .fuga prohibet: nos vivimus,* 13. 28. 2 *quam enim turpis est adsentatio, cum vivere ipsum turpe sit nobis,* 14. 9. 2 *itaque quam severe nos M. Curtius accusat, ut pudeat vivere, neque iniuria.* Cf. Quint. *Inst.* 6. pr. 14 *nemo nisi sua culpa diu dolet. sed vivimus.*

4. 7. 2   de Metello, οὐχ ὁσίη φθιμένοισιν, sed tamen multis annis civis nemo erat mortuus *qui quidem* —. tibi nummi meo periculo sint. quid enim vereris? quemcumque heredem fecit, nisi Publium fecit, virum fecit non improbiorem quam fuit ipse. quare in hoc thecam nummariam non retexeris, in aliis eris cautior.

qui *bds,* quid *MmNORP*   verum fecit non improbi (-be *Mms*) quemquam (quamquam *s*) Ω, *corr. Müller*

This aposiopesis is insufferable. 'Fort. audiendum *minus est desiderandus* vel *peior* vel simile quid', Purser: but then why *quidem*? After a relative pronoun *quidem* emphasizes the relative clause, either restricting the main statement, as in 7. 2. 3 *epistulas. . . aliam alia iucundiorem, quae quidem erant tua manu,* or adding a new and important point. The main clause has to be complete in itself. Perhaps *cui equidem* — [sc. εὐχετάασθαι, *insultare malim*].

Below, Müller's reading, followed by Constans, is perhaps the best the case admits. Cicero's meaning is thus far pretty certain, that Metellus' heir cannot be more unscrupulous than Metellus himself. 'Therefore', he continues, 'you won't have to open your coffer for this purpose [or 'in his case']', i.e. 'you won't get your money back'. If, as is always assumed, Metellus owed Atticus money, there seems to be no other possible way of understanding *thecam non retexeris,* which can only signify the putting of money in or the taking of money out. But this discouraging prophecy nullifies the preceding assurance that Atticus' money is safe because Metellus' heir can hardly be a greater rogue than Metellus himself.

Suppose the debt was due, not from Metellus to Atticus, but the other way round. So, and only so, the sentence will hang together. I imagine the circumstances, which were doubtless explained in Atticus' letter if Cicero did not know them before, as follows. Metellus had a claim on Atticus, perhaps based on a legal quibble, which Metellus himself had not cared to take into court; now that he is dead Atticus is afraid his heir may pursue the matter. Cicero reassures him: 'Don't worry. Metellus' heir is not likely to prove a greater rascal than Metellus himself. So you will not have to loosen your purse strings for this purpose.'

4. 8a. 3   de poemate quod quaeris, quid si cupiat effugere? quid? *sinat?*

Editors read *sinas* (Manutius). Perhaps there is not much to choose between this and *sinam*, but I prefer the latter as the more direct—the decision being properly Cicero's. Cf. 9. 2a. 1 *quid si hoc ipso premar? accipiam?*

4. 11. 1   dixit mihi Pompeius Crassum a se in Albano exspectari ante diem IIII Kal.; is cum venisset, Romam *et se* statim venturos.

esse is attributed to Kayser, who in fact proposed *esse se*.[1] Manutius in 1540 read *Romam esse statim venturos.* Modern editors find Lehmann's ⟨*eum*⟩ *et se* an improvement, unaware that the speaker should have precedence. Cardinal Wolsey knew better, so I learned at school. Perhaps *et se* ⟨*et eum*⟩.

4. 15. 4 (27 July 54)   a. d. IIII Non. Quint. Sufenas et Cato absoluti, Procilius condemnatus. ex quo intellectum est τρισαρεοπαγίτας ambitum, comitia, interregnum, maiestatem, totam denique rem publicam flocci non facere, patrem familias domi suae occidi nolle, neque tamen id ipsum abunde; nam absolverunt XXII, condemnarunt XXVIII. Publius sane diserto epilogo *criminans* mentes iudicum moverat. Hortalus in ea causa fuit

---

[1] In the Adnotatio Critica prefixed to vol. x of Baiter–Kayser's edition (p. xxi)—Professor Watt's reference.

cuiusmodi solet. nos verbum nullum; verita est enim pusilla, quae nunc laborat, ne animum Publii offenderet.

epilogo criminans mentes M^2N, epilogo cruminarmentes M, epilogotium marmentes P, epilogo criminari mentes Δ (*praeter M*) O, in R epilogocrum in armentes *legit Constans* (epilogarum *Moricca*)

Even if Clodius was prosecuting, as editors suppose, *criminans* (sc. *eum, reum*[1]) would be odd. What else should a prosecutor do but *criminari*? However, it is far more likely that he spoke for the defence.

One reason for thinking so is that Cicero's attitude towards Procilius was evidently unsympathetic: 'these juries of ours do, it seems, draw the line at the murder of a man in his own house'. He is twice mentioned elsewhere: 4. 16. 5 *de Procilio rumores non boni, sed iudicia nosti.* This implies that Procilius ought to be convicted, though, juries being what they were, he might get off (*non boni*, 'sinister rumours', is only mock concern): and *Q. Fr.* 2. 7 (6). 1 *Id. Maiis senatus frequens divinus fuit in supplicatione Gabinio deneganda. adiurat Procilius hoc nemini accidisse.* Whether or not Procilius approved of the insult to Gabinius is not stated; but his comment would hardly have been worth repeating unless it was in opposition to the general sentiment, i.e. a protest against Gabinius' treatment.

The incongruity of Clodius accusing a man whom Cicero disliked is strengthened by the nature of the case. Procilius was presumably a colleague of Sufenas and C. Cato in the tribunate of 56, concerned like them in the holding up of the elections that year on behalf of Pompey and Crassus.[2] For Clodius to prosecute him in that connection would not make political sense. C. Cato, moreover, was an old enemy of Cicero and Milo (*Q. Fr.* 2. 4. 5), though recently reconciled (4. 16. 5), and an ally of Clodius (*Q. Fr.* 2. 1. 2). Finally the statement *Publius...moverat* reads to my mind most naturally as an explanation of the size of the vote for acquittal.

Madvig's ⟨*me*⟩ *criminans* is possible, but I do not find it convincing. Apart from Cicero's apparent irrelevance to the case, it is not like him to mention a point against himself in this casual fashion.

---

[1] Sternkopf, *Hermes*, 1905, pp. 26 f.
[2] See *RE*, *Nonius* 52 and *Porcius* 6.

criminans should be *lacrimans*—*la* falling out, *crimans* or *crumans* (cf. M) would easily be taken for *crīnans*. Tears in a Roman peroration *ad misericordiam* were well within the rules: cf. *De Or.* 190, with Wilkins' note.

4. 16. 9 nihil videbatur esse in quo tantulum interesset utrum per procuratores ageres an per te ipsum *mutabis totiens* et tam longe abesses.

ut ab iis totiens *cod. Faerni*

The established reading *ut ab his tot tuis* (Sternkopf, comparing 4. 15. 2) should be discarded in favour of *ut a tuis totiens* (Boot: so Winstedt) or *ut a nobis totiens* (Baiter). An adverb of time is wanted to balance *longe*, and for *totiens abesses* cf. Prop. 4. 3. 2 *cum totiens absis*, Ov. *Her.* 19. 70 *cur totiens a me, lente morator, abes?*

4. 17. 1 quae [*sc.* epistulae] tantum habent mysteriorum ut eas ne librariis quidem fere committamus *lepidum quo* excidat.

ne quid umquam (Starker) is adopted by Constans, but it seems best to retain *quo*, as several conjectures do: *lepidum quid ne quo excidat* (Tyrrell: 'id erat scilicet verendum', Müller), *trepidi, num quo excidant* (Fr. Schmidt), *ne quid divini quo* (Constans), *ne quid aliquo* (Müller). The last has merit, but I prefer *ne quid quo*: cf. 5. 11. 5 *nec mehercule habeo quod adhuc quem accusem meorum*, 6. 1. 20 *num quid de quo inaudisti?*, 11. 13. 5 *si quid erit quod ad quos scribendum meo nomine putes*, 12. 14. 3 *non quo proficiam quid*.

4. 17. 4 (1 Oct. 54) ibi [*sc.* in senatu] loquetur praeter *Antium* et Favonium libere nemo; nam Cato aegrotat.

The Antii of whom there is record at this period are hardly more than shadows. That speech of Sestius which gave Catullus a cold was *in Antium petitorem* (Cat. 44. 7 ff.), and Appian speaks of an Antius among the proscribed in 43 (*B.C.* 4. 40). Ampius, the *tuba belli civilis*, comes to mind, since *t* and *p* are easily confused; but he was a staunch adherent of Pompey, and so hardly qualifies for a place in this free-spoken trinity. Much more likely is C. Ateius Capito, best remembered for his cursing of Crassus. Dio (39. 32) mentions him and another as the only tribunes who upheld the senatorial

party against the consuls in 55, and again (39. 35) as supporting Cato
and Favonius in opposition. *ateium* would become *ātium* all the more
easily because the copyist had met the town Antium in two preceding letters of this book.

BOOK V

5. 10. 5 valde me Athenae delectarunt, urbe dumtaxat et urbis
ornamento et hominum amore in te, in nos quadam benevolentia.

amore *C*: amores *Ω* (*praet. N*), mores *M^cN*   et *post* te *add. C*

in te et in nos is the vulgate, but *et* is best away. It spoils the antithesis between *amore* and *quadam benevolentia*.

5. 12. 2 de Messalla *ad te* statim ut audivi de Gyaro dedi litteras *et
id ipsum* consilium nostrum etiam ad Hortensium, cui quidem
valde συνηγωνίων.

Madvig[1] maintains justly that a letter of congratulation to Messalla
is what Cicero would naturally have written on the news of his
acquittal, rather than a letter to Atticus about Messalla. But his *ad
Messallam auctore te* [vel sim.] *statim* is violent, and Tyrrell's *a te*
insufficient. Instead of inserting *ad eum* after *litteras* (TP, not holding this indispensable however), I take *a te* from Tyrrell (or *autem*
from Watt) and *ad* from Corradus,[2] thus: *de Messalla a te statim ut
audivi de Gyaro dedi litteras et ad ipsum et* (*id consilium nostrum*)
etiam ad Hortensium. The parenthesis[3] I understand to mean 'that
was *my* idea', Atticus having suggested a letter to Messalla. Professor Watt suggests *vide* for *id*. For *et...etiam* cf. *Fam.* 9. 25. 3
auctoritate tua nobis opus est et consilio et etiam gratia, 15. 4. 13 *et
natura et magis etiam...ratione atque doctrina et* sim.

5. 13. 3 exhauri mea mandata maximeque, si quid potest, de illo
domestico scrupulo quem non ignoras, dein de Caesare, *cum* in
cupiditatem te auctore incubui, nec me piget.

---

[1] *Adv.* III, p. 175.   [2] '*et ad ipsum* libet legere' is all he says.
[3] Madvig first saw that a parenthesis is required. He read *id ipsum consilium
nostrum*.

For *cum* everyone reads *cuius* (so first, apparently, Victorius), which must be understood 'and on your suggestion I am eagerly desirous of this' (TP)—'this' being the repayment of Caesar's loan. But *cuius* (neut.) comes awkwardly after *Caesare*, which looks like the antecedent and has actually been so taken. *quam* would be better Latin—better palaeography too, for *cum* is far more commonly confused with *quam* than with *cuius* (examples in 2. 10, 2. 11. 1, 2. 18. 3, 3. 24. 1, 7. 3. 10, 11. 12. 1).

ibid.   de aqua, *si curae est*, si quid Philippus aget, animadvertes.

si cur(a)e *ΔO*, sciture *RP*, scitur *G*, si tui *N*

The Latin of the vulgate is clumsy, and the sense hardly more than nonsense. Better to rewrite with Boot *de aqua tibi curae esto* [*sit* in his first edition]. *quid Philippus agat, animadvertes*; but the same result can be more economically gained: *de aqua si⟨t⟩ curae; et si quid* et sqq.

5. 16. 3   concursus fiunt ex agris, ex vicis, *ex nominibus ex omnibus.*
        mehercule etiam adventu nostro reviviscunt.

ex domibus ex omnibus *ms*

Ernesti's *ex oppidis omnibus* should be accepted and Liv. 37. 54. 15 *illi agrum, hi vicos, hi oppida, hi portus...ut possideant* compared.[1] Editors prefer *ex domibus omnibus* (edd. vett.), an absurd exaggeration which spoils the series (in ascending order of population) 'country, villages, towns', but better than *ex domibus ex omnibus* (in TP's text) or *ex domibus* (Gurlitt, as though villages did not contain houses).

In the next sentence *et* (Lambinus) should probably precede *mehercule*,[2] but there is no need to alter *etiam* to *iam*.[3]

---

[1] Professor Watt points to *Pis.* 51 *quid dicam adventus meos, quid effusiones hominum ex oppidis, quid concursus ex agris patrum familias cum coniugibus ac liberis, Post Red. in Sen.* 24 *ut...senatus omnes ex omnibus agris atque oppidis cives...excitaret, Flacc.* 74 *qui concursus ex oppidis finitimis undique?, Leg. Man.* 38 *per agros atque oppida.*

[2] See on 16. 6. 2.

[3] See on 5. 12. 2.

5. 18. 4 faciam tamen satis, *tibi quidem*, cui difficilius est quam ipsi: sed certe satis faciam utrique.

Cicero means 'satisfaction shall be given, and given to you, which is more difficult than giving it to Brutus himself'. He would normally express that by writing *et quidem tibi* or *et (ac) tibi quidem*: cf. 9. 8. 1 *cenantibus* 11 *Id. nobis ac noctu quidem, Fin.* 4. 74 *et regna nata vobis sunt et imperia et divitiae et tantae quidem ut* et sqq., and many more examples in Krebs–Schmalz, *Antibarbarus*, 1, p. 523. If any change is required ⟨*et*⟩ *tibi* is as likely as *cui quidem* (usually attributed to Wesenberg, but Professor Watt points out that it appears in the text of R. Stephanus)—I will not say more likely, for either corruption would be commonplace. The text can however be defended by 9. 1. 3 *in conviviis, tempestivis quidem* and a few passages in later prose, Val. Max. 9. 5. 3 fin., Tac. *Ann.* 2. 38. 4, Suet. *Claud.* 46 *aliquot quidem argumentis.*

5. 19. 3 (September 51) quod scribis libente te repulsam tulisse eum qui cum sororis tuae filii patruo *certaret*, magni amoris signum.

libente te Lipsius: libenter Ω

certaret is open to an objection which also rules out *certarit* (Ernesti) and *certasset* (R. Klotz). The subjunctive attributes the whole sequence *libente...certaret* to Atticus, who must be supposed to have written *libente me repulsam tulit is qui cum sororis meae filii patruo certat*. The facetious paraphrase is pointless in Atticus' mouth, and the parallel in 6. 8. 3 *sed heus tu, numquid moleste fers de illo qui se solet anteferre patruo sororis tuae filii* practically stamps it as a piece of mock modesty on Cicero's part. In that case an indicative is required.

What indicative? That depends on who is referred to. If, as used to be supposed, it is C. Lucilius Hirrus, who had unsuccessfully contested the augurate with Cicero in 53 and failed this year as a candidate for the curule aedileship, Lambinus' *certarat* is satisfactory. But TP and Constans rightly take Moll's view that M. Calidius is intended, a noted orator of the Atticizing school whose defeat in the consular elections this year is mentioned in *Fam.* 8. 4. 1.[1] The

---

[1] Münzer in *RE*, III, 1354 agrees, but goes back to Hirrus in XIII, 1643 f. This, like the reading *certavit* in his citation, may be no more than inadvertence.

decisive point is the similarity of phrasing in 6. 8. 3 (of October 50), which practically forces us to understand the same man in both passages. Now it could hardly be said of Hirrus that he was in the habit (*solet*) of placing himself above Cicero, nor is he likely to have met with another electoral rebuff in 50. Calidius may easily have failed a second time for the consulate and, in his own estimation, he may have been a better orator than Cicero.

If Calidius is the man, *certarat*, which could only apply to a particular contest, will not do. 6. 8. 3 suggests *certare ⟨sole⟩t*. As will appear, I cannot claim 10. 4. 11 *facere ⟨sole⟩t* as a parallel corruption.

5. 20. 5   hilara sane Saturnalia militibus quoque, quibus exceptis reliquam praedam concessimus. mancipia venibant Saturnalibus tertiis.

quibus *M²NORP*, equibus (*superscr.* equis *M^c*) *M*, equis *bdms*

Horses appear in most texts down to 1870, and have been restored by Winstedt and Constans, who have *quibus ⟨equis⟩ exceptis* after Baiter. Wesenberg's[1] two arguments to the contrary are of unequal force. It is certainly unlikely that horses should have been found in quantity at a mountain stronghold like Pindenissus. It might be possible, on the other hand, for Cicero to say that all the booty except the horses went to the soldiers, and then to add that the slaves were sold for the state, if he regarded the captive population as apart from the booty: cf. Liv. 7. 27. 8 *praeda omnis militi data. extra praedam quattuor milia deditorum habita; eos vinctos consul ante currum triumphans egit; venditis deinde, magnam pecuniam in aerarium redegit.* But *equis* becomes even less plausible if attention is given to the normal Roman practice in such cases. What this was appears from a series of passages in Livy of which 23. 37. 12 will serve as a specimen: *ex Hirpinis oppida tria, quae a populo Romano defecerant, vi recepta...supra quinque milia captivorum sub hasta venierunt; praeda alia militi concessa.* That is the usual pattern whenever a town or camp is taken by storm; the people are slaughtered, or kept in custody for a triumph, or sold then and there. It is repeated with a few minor variations in 4. 34. 4, 5. 21. 17, 6. 13. 6, 7. 27. 8, 10. 31. 4,

[1] *Emend.* p. 37.

24. 16. 5, 43. 19. 12, also Tac. *Ann.* 13. 39. 7. One exception: after the battle of Sutrium (?) in 310 the enemy's gold and silver was brought to the consul. Hannibal after Cannae, it is true, reserved the Roman captives, horses, and silver.

Unless *exceptis* be deleted (Wesenberg's original proposal, followed by Boot, ed. 1) the choice virtually lies between the supplements *captivis* (Wesenberg) and *mancipiis* (Tyrrell). Müller and Sjögren take the second; the first is better. Most of the captives would not be slaves until the Romans made them so. It is natural for Cicero to write *mancipia venibant*, but less natural for him to call them so before any mention of the auction.

5. 20. 7   sed est totum, quid Kal. Mart. futurum sit.

Koch's addition *in eo* after *totum* (half anticipated by Boot in 1865) restores Latin; cf. Müller ad loc. But *sed est totum ⟨in eo situm⟩* or *⟨in eo positum⟩* explains the lacuna—by 'parablepsy'. Cf. 12. 27. 1 *est enim totum positum in te*, 13. 32. 1 *in eo enim totum est positum id quod cogitamus*, 7. 9. 4 *quo consilio, in temporibus situm est.* Similarly in 11. 7. 5, better *totum ⟨in eo est positum⟩* than *totum ⟨in eo est⟩* or *⟨in eo est⟩ totum.* I do not mean to imply that *in eo (est)* might not easily drop out without any 'mechanical' explanation.

BOOK VI

6. 1. 8   οὐκ ἔλαθέ σ⟨ε⟩ illud de gestu histrionis. tu sceleste suspicaris, ego ἀφελῶς scripsi.

οὐκ ἔλαθε…*histrionis* is a question: 'So you cottoned on, did you…?', quoting something in Atticus' letter (οὐκ ἔλαθέ με…). It cannot be a statement, because Cicero goes on to deny that there was any ulterior meaning to discover.

6. 1. 13   haec non noram tum cum Democrito tuo locutus sum

tamen cum *M²N*

Modern editors follow Lambinus: *tum cum Democrito tuo ⟨cum⟩ locutus sum*, in order to avoid the un-Ciceronian *tum cum ⟨cum⟩*.[1]

---

[1] See Lehmann, *Quaest. Tull.* pp. 106 ff.

But the prepositional *cum* where, after *tum*, the reader expects a conjunction, displeases. On diplomatic grounds too Lehmann's disregarded alternative *tum ⟨cum de ea re* [or *de eo*]⟩ *cum* is at least as good. But *de ea re* or *de eo* makes it necessary to suppose that the Terentius mentioned a few lines earlier is Atticus' runaway slave, which is not very probable.[1] So perhaps *tum ⟨cum illa⟩ cum* is to be preferred. For the accusative cf., for example, 6. 8. 2 *cum Lepta etiam plura locutus est.*

6. 1. 16 itaque et Graeci solvunt tolerabili faenore et publicanis res est gratissima, *si* illa iam habent pleno modio, verborum honorem, invitationem crebram.

si om. RP

sic, sibi . . . habeant, scilicet, and *sed* have been conjectured. But *si* is causal, =*siquidem* (*illa* being anticipatory). Examples in Kühner–Stegmann II, 427 f. are hardly to the point, but cf. *Fam.* 11. 5. 1 *qua re hortatione tu quidem non eges, si ne in illa quidem re, quae a te gesta est post hominum memoriam maxima, hortatorem desiderasti.*

6. 2. 1 I read and punctuate thus:

et respondebo primum postremae tuae paginae, *qua* mihi magnae molestiae fuit quod ad te scriptum est a Cincio de Statii sermone. in quo hoc molestissimum est, Statium dicere a me quoque id consilium probari. de isto *autem* hactenus dixerim, me vel plurima vincla tecum summae coniunctionis optare *et sqq.*

qua *scripsi*: quae Ω   de isto autem *cod. Helmstadiensis*: autem de isto Ω

For *qua* cf. 8. 9. 1 *qua autem est 'aliquid impertias temporis'.*

de isto autem may be right; the vulgate *quod ad te scriptum est . . . id consilium probari—⟨probari⟩ autem?—, de isto* et sqq. is certainly wrong. When *autem* is so used in a question which repeats a preceding word in order to correct it, the correction must follow. Normally the word or phrase to be substituted follows immediately, as e.g. in *Fam.* 1. 9. 10 *inimicum meum—meum autem? immo vero legum, iudiciorum, . . . bonorum omnium.* See *T.L.L.* II, 1579. 57–69.

[1] See Münzer, *RE*, VA, 592 f.

6. 2. 3 Graecos in eo reprehendit quod *mare tam* secuti sunt

maretani *N*, mare tum O^2

It is very doubtful whether Cicero ever has *tam*=*tantopere* unless followed by *quam* or in a negative clause. In 14. 8. 1 *iam* is often read for *tam*. In 13. 25. 3 *male mi sit si umquam quicquam tam enitar*, *male mi sit si umquam* is practically *numquam*; perhaps, though, *tam* should be *tantum*. So here Orelli's *tantum* is read by Müller. I should prefer *maritima* (see the context).

6. 2. 5 mira erant in civitatibus ipsorum furta Graecorum, quae magistratus ⟨s⟩ui fecerant. quaesivi ipse de iis qui annis decem proximis magistratum gesserant. aperte fatebantur. itaque sine ulla ignominia *suis umeris* pecunias populis rettulerunt. populi autem nullo gemitu publicanis, quibus hoc ipso lustro nihil solverant, etiam superioris lustri reddiderunt.

I see nothing strange in *suis umeris*, bearing in mind that *pecunias* meant in effect bags of coin. *suis umeris referre* is perfectly good Latin (cf. *Dom.* 40 *dicebas te tuis umeris me custodem urbis in urbem relaturum*, *Post. Red. in Sen.* 39 *cum me . . . Italia cuncta paene suis umeris reportarit*), and the hyperbole, *suis umeris* for *sua sponte*, an agreeable touch. Purser's *ex* (or *de*) *suis crumenis* should disappear from apparatus. Nor is there any need for explanations like Bayet's 'l'image peut se référer à des jeux de scène comiques et à des attitudes d'esclaves (cf. par ex., PLAUTE, Asin. 277, 657 s., 661 . . .)'.

Modern texts add *reliqua* (Wesenberg) after *lustri*, perhaps rightly. But I do not find it too hard to understand this, as earlier editors did, from the context.

6. 5. 3 cum . . . ad meque legati eius et quaestor et amici *eius* litteras mitterent.

eius (*post* amici) *om. E*

Some editors omit the second *eius* with E ('an *mandatu eius?*' Müller), but cf. *Inv.* 2. 117 *ex ceteris eius scriptis et ex factis, dictis, animo atque vita eius*, Nep. *Eum.* 13. 4 *ossaque eius in Cappadociam ad matrem atque uxorem liberosque eius deportanda curarunt*, Liv. 3. 7. 2 *eorum . . . eorum*. Professor Watt points to *Fam.* 13. 21. 2 *domum eius . . . libertum eius* as the nearest example in the Letters.

BOOK VII

7. 1. 3 haec enim cogitabamus, nec mihi coniuncto cum Pompeio
fore necesse peccare in re publica aliquando nec cum *Pompeio*
sentienti pugnandum esse cum *Caesare.* tanta erat illorum
coniunctio.

Malaespina's transposition *cum Caesare sentienti*...*cum Pompeio*
has been the vulgate for so long that it seems to have acquired
squatter's rights in conservative eyes. It is a palaeographically
violent change, neither necessary to the sense nor even, in my
judgment, plausible intrinsically. Did Cicero ever quite envisage
himself as *cum Caesare sentientem*, words which in this context can
only refer to politics? Why not let him say that in cultivating Pompey
and Caesar he had felt justified by two considerations?—(*a*) Pompey
being fundamentally a good citizen, friendship with him would
never entail disloyalty to the state. (*b*) Alliance with Pompey could
not be combined with hostility to Caesar—they were too close to
one another to allow of that. In other words, alliance with Pompey
was a safe plan for a patriot, and the abandonment of enmity with
Caesar its unavoidable corollary. It might be suggested that the
second *Pompeio* is a gloss upon *eo*; but even that is unlikely, cf.
Sjögren, *Comm. Tull.* pp. 160 f.

7. 1. 8 redeo ad Hirrum. coeperas eum mihi placare; perfice.
habes Scrofam, habes Silium. ad eos ego *etiam* antea scripsi, et
iam ad ipsum Hirrum.

et iam] etiam *P, om. Δ*

No doubt *etiam* could be an anticipation of *et iam*, as Sjögren[1]
maintains, but I see no reason why it should not be genuine. Cicero
says he had written to Scrofa and Silius 'even before', i.e. before he
knew of Hirrus' conciliatory behaviour in the debate. The purpose
of the letters, it is implied, was to ask them to promote peace with
Hirrus. Now, after the news of the debate, he has written to Hirrus
himself.

[1] Χάριτες *F. Leo,* pp. 286 ff.

7. 2. 3   Tironem Patris aegrum reliqui, adulescentem ut nosti et adde, si quid vis, probum.

It is a question whether *doctum* (Wesenberg) should be added after *adulescentem*. Other occurrences of *ut nosti [noras]* in Cicero do not justify *ut nosti* [sc. *eum*]=*qualem nosti*: cf. 4. 16. 3 *ioculatorem senem illum, ut noras*, 16. 16A. 5 *erat enim popularis, ut noras, Fam.* 13. 10. 2 *cum ingenio, ut nosti.* But in the case of a colloquial usage this is not a conclusive objection. How suspicious we should be of 13. 10. 3 *illum, ut erat, constantius respondisse* if we did not happen to have a parallel, apparently unique, in *Fam.* 12. 20 *quod si, ut es, cessabis* ! Petr. 67. 1 is somewhat similar '*quomodo nosti*', inquit, '*illam*', Trimalchio, '*nisi argentum composuerit, . . . aquam in os suum non coniciet.*' There is weight too in the analogies from *Q. Fr.* cited by TP.[1]

Müller's punctuation *adulescentem, ut nosti (et adde, si quid vis), probum* is certainly to be rejected. All analogy shows that *probum* must be taken with *adde*. Besides Hor. *Sat.* 2. 7. 39 *imbecillus, iners, si quid vis, adde popino* cf. 6. 1. 13 *adde M. Nonium, Bibulum, me si voles, Off.* 1. 150 *adde huc, si placet, unguentarios, Clu.* 89 *adde etiam illud, si placet, Fin.* 2. 89 *addam, si vis, animi, De Or.* 2. 65 *addat, si quis volet, etiam laudationes,* Sen. *Dial.* 7. 17. 2 *adice, si vis, cur trans mare possides,* 11. 3. 1 *adiciamus, si vis, ad has querelas ipsius adulescentis interceptam inter prima incrementa indolem, Ep.* 81. 3 *adice, si vis, et illud,* [Quint.] *Decl.* 298 (Ritter, 174. 29) *et adice, si vis, meretrice.* For *si quid vis*=*si vis* add to Hor. loc. cit. Petr. 58. 8 *ad summam, si quid vis, ego et tu sponsiunculam.*

Somebody will point out one day if I do not do it now that the omission of *et* makes *adulescentem. . .probum* into an iambic trimeter.

7. 3. 7   sed in hoc genere, si modo per rem p. licebit, non accusabimur posthac, neque hercule antea neglegentes fuimus sed *et amicorum* multitudine occupati.

It is not like Cicero to say that he was kept busy by the number of his friends, i.e. by his legal work, without also mentioning the cares of state: cf. *Fam.* 4. 6. 2 *non amicorum negotiis, non rei publicae procuratione impediebantur cogitationes meae,*[1] *De Or.* 1. 3 *quantum mihi vel fraus inimicorum vel causae amicorum vel res publica tribuet otii,* 1. 78 *nos . . . quos in foro, quos in ambitione, quos in re publica, quos in amicorum negotiis res ipsa ante confecit,* 2. 24 *quando ages negotium publicum? quando amicorum?, Off.* 2. 4 *quantum superfuerat amicorum et rei publicae temporibus,* Plin. *Ep.* 3. 5. 19 *quem partim publica, partim amicorum officia distringunt.* So, while agreeing with Sjögren in the retention of *et*, which earlier editors discard, I would prefer ⟨*et in re p.*⟩ *et amicorum* to his *et amicorum* ⟨*et alienorum*⟩.

7. 3. 8   de serpirastris cohortis meae nihil ⟨est⟩ quod doleas. ipsi enim se collegerunt admiratione integritatis meae. sed me moverat nemo magis quam is, quem tu *nemo* putas. idem et initio fuerat et nunc est egregius. sed in ipsa decessione significavit sperasse se aliquid et id quod animum induxerat paulisper non tenuit, sed cito ad se rediit meisque honorificentissimis erga se officiis victus pluris ea duxit quam omnem pecuniam.

It is hard to see what attraction editors have found in *neminem* (Aldus) to compensate for the lack of any MS. authority, unless it be bad Latin or bad sense. Neither Cicero nor any other classical writer says *nemo* when he means *nihili*; and it is improbable that he should have been so much disturbed or distressed (*moverat*) by the behaviour of any but one member of his staff, namely his brother Quintus.[2] It would be like him to avoid the name in such a context. So when the younger Quintus is in disgrace his uncle is apt to call him *quidam* or *sororis tuae filius.* Now we know that Quintus did later on complain of ungenerous treatment in Cilicia (11. 13. 4).

What is to be done with *nemo?* Manutius' explanation of *neminem putas* as *minime omnium putas* makes better sense but no less incredible Latin than the one usually given. *nemo* probably comes from the previous *nemo*: cf. e.g. 10. 17. 1, where *scripta* from foregoing *scripsisse* replaces *lecta* in all MSS. (see Müller, pp. x–xii).

---

[1] Cf. Sulpicius Rufus in *Fam.* 4. 5. 3 (which 4. 6. 2 answers) *in republica, in amicorum negotiis libertate sua usuri?*

[2] The quaestor Mescinius can be eliminated; see TP.

Perhaps *minime*[1] (Watt) should be substituted, perhaps simply *non*.
Atticus may have written that Quintus anyhow would give no
trouble.

7. 3. 9　Hortensi legata cognovi. nunc aveo scire quid *hominis* sit et
　　　quarum rerum auctionem instituat.

This is intelligible if *quid hominis sit* means 'what belongs to the
fellow', i.e. the younger Hortensius (see TP). There are two objec-
tions. (*a*) *Hortensi legata* more naturally means 'the legacies left by
Hortensius (the father)' than 'the legacies payable by Hortensius
(the son)'. But if *Hortensi* is the father, it is difficult though not
impossible for *hominis* to be the son.[2] (*b*) *quid hominis sit* elsewhere
means 'what sort of a fellow he is': see *T.L.L.* VI. 3, 2888. 58–63.
Perhaps *hominis* (*hoīs*) should be *heredis* (*h̄dis*): 'I have heard about
Hortensius' legacies; now I am longing to hear what belongs to the
heir, and what he is going to put up for auction.' Hortensius, despite
threats to disinherit his son, did in fact make him his heir (Val. Max.
5. 9. 2).

7. 6. 2 (c. 18 December 50)　de re p. valde timeo nec adhuc fere in-
　　　veni qui non concedendum putaret Caesari quod postularet
　　　potius quam depugnandum. est illa quidem impudens postu-
　　　latio, *opinione valentior*. cur autem nunc primum ei resistamus?

impudens *om. M* (*add. M*²) *bs*

If *autem* is adversative, answering *quidem*, *valentior* is impossible.
For in that case the protasis must contain reasons for rejecting
Caesar's demands. Moreover *postulatio valens*, 'a demand backed by
power', is hardly Latin. The proposed corrections *violentior* (Koch)
and *amentior* (Schmidt), with or without Wesenberg's *atque* before
opinione, give unsatisfactory sense. Caesar's claim to stand for the
consulship while retaining his command was impudent, from
Cicero's point of view (and Pompey's, cf. 7. 9. 4), because it

---

[1] I had preferred *nullus* (as in *nullus creduas* et sim.), as likely to have baffled
a copyist. But the resemblance of *nime* to *nemo* speaks for *minime*.
[2] 7. 2. 7 *Hortensius quid egerit aveo scire, Cato quid agat* is none too clear.
I take the first question to mean 'what Hortensius [the elder] has done [in his
will]'.

demanded a concession by threat of force; but no one who had followed the manœuvres of the past two years was likely to be surprised by its violence or insanity. There remains Lehmann's supplement ⟨*sed is qui postulat*⟩. This is very neat diplomatically, and 7. 3. 4–5 lays emphasis on the political strength built up by Caesar. But was this greater than people expected?[1] And is *postularet* ...*postulatio*...*postulat* not too much of a good word? I do not feel wholly content, though if the next editor puts Lehmann's conjecture in place of a nonsensical vulgate I shall not complain.

In the meantime a different line of correction may be worth considering. To the public opinion which Cicero here describes as favouring concession to Caesar his claims may have appeared not more but less exorbitant than might have been expected. Appian's account (*B.C.* 2. 31) of the panic which a month or so previously had followed a report that Caesar had crossed the Alps and was marching on the capital suggests that many would not have been surprised if he had returned to Rome as Marius did in 87. As it was, lovers of peace could tell themselves that he was asking no more than might have been granted to any commander who enjoyed the Senate's confidence and less than had been granted to Pompey in 52. Perhaps then *opinione tamen lenior*. Caesar himself speaks of his *lenissima postulata* in *B.C.* 1. 5. 5.

cur autem then (as with Lehmann) adds another argument for concession. Why resist now after yielding so much in the past?

ibid.   dicam idem quod Pompeius, neque id faciam humili animo.
         sed rursus hoc permagnum rei p. malum *est, et* quodam modo
         mihi praeter ceteros non rectum, me in tantis rebus a Pompeio
         dissidere.
                         et *om. E*

'*hoc*] the necessity imposed on the *boni* to "say ditto" to Pompey', TP. Perhaps so, but the thought is obscurely expressed. There would be a gain in lucidity if we read *malum, esse quodam modo*: 'but here is another very great public misfortune, that I more than others am in a way morally debarred from disagreement with

---

[1] I do not think *omnes qui aere alieno premantur, quos pluris esse intellego quam putaram* really supports this idea. *pluris* (gen. sing.)...*putaram* is a jest.

Pompey in matters of such consequence'. He implies that he would have been the most powerful advocate of moderation, which he thinks to be to the public good, if only he had not been muzzled by personal obligation to Pompey. On *me* (secl. Boot) v. Madvig, *Fin.* 3. 10.

7. 11. 5 (19 Jan. 49)   te puto iam videre quae sit ὁρμὴ Caesaris, qui populus, qui totius negotii status.

ὁρμὴ *Victorius*: hora me *vel sim.* Ω

ὁρμή is usually taken in its philosophical sense, *appetitio qua ad agendum impellimur* (*Acad.* 2. 24); hence 'aim', 'motive'. Why should Cicero want or expect information from Atticus about Caesar's motives? They were already only too plain: τὴν θεῶν μεγίστην ὥστ᾽ ἔχειν τυραννίδα (§1). What he would want to know the day after he left Rome, and what Atticus, still there, might be able to tell him, was the direction in which Caesar was moving. ὁρμή='forward rush', *impetus* (cf. 8. 3. 4 *impetu huius belli*). The usual absurd misinterpretation, in which certain early scholars did not share, originated in Victorius' note. He actually quotes in its favour Dio 41. 5. 2 πρέσβεις πρὸς τὸν Καίσαρα... ἀπέστειλεν, εἴ πως τὴν ὁρμὴν αὐτοῦ ἐκφυγὼν ἔπειτ᾽ ἐπὶ μετρίοις τισὶ συμβαίη.[1] *qua* [sc. *via*] might replace *quae* with advantage.

7. 18. 1   quae quidem [*sc.* responsa Pompei] ille si repudiarit, iacebit; *si acceperit,* —. 'utrum igitur', inquies, 'mavis?' responderem, si quemadmodum parati essemus scirem.

ille si *P, cod. Faerni*: ille ΔNOR

The sense ought to be obvious from 7. 9. 3 and 7. 15. 3 *vicerit enim, si consul factus erit, et minore scelere vicerit quam quo ingressus est,* and apparently was so to Corradus.[2] If Caesar makes peace on terms which grant him the consulship he will have won the game, whereas a refusal will discredit him. Which then should men of good will be hoping for? That depends on whether the Pompeians are equipped to fight. TP's note is a tangle of misunderstanding.

[1] So I think his note must be understood; but it is not altogether lucid, and he does mention that ὁρμή sometimes has the other meaning.

[2] His note reads 'si acceperit] minore scelere vicerit. ep. 14 [i.e. 15] h.l. alii, si acceperit? ut sit ἀποσιώπησις, quid erit?'

I can see no good reason why the apodosis *vicerit* should have been left to Atticus' imagination. It is much more likely to have fallen out of the text after *acceperit*.

7. 18. 3   de Dionysio...ita constitui, exspectare responsa Caesaris, ut, si ad urbem rediremus, ibi nos exspectaret, sin tardius id fieret, tum eum arcesseremus. omnino quid ille facere debuerit in nostra illa fuga, quid docto homine et amico dignum fuerit, cum praesertim rogatus esset, scio, sed haec non nimis exquiro a Graecis. tu tamen videbis, *si* erit, quod nolim, arcessendus, ne molesti simus invito.

No one seems to have been incommoded by the fatuity of the last sentence. Cicero hopes it will not be necessary to send for the reluctant tutor; but if that does become necessary, how in the name of friendship and common sense is Atticus going to take care not to trouble an unwilling man? It is just possible that Cicero's pen here outran his wits. More probable, I think, that he wrote *nisi*. Dionysius *ought* to come of his own accord, of course. However, one can't expect much from a Greek. At all events he is not to be pestered to come against his will, unless it should unfortunately become necessary to send for him. *simus* associates Atticus in the matter because Dionysius was Atticus' protégé, and Cicero expected his friend to share his own concern and disappointment (9. 15. 5 *te medius fidius hanc rem gravius putavi laturum esse quam me*). When Dionysius finally arrived at Formiae Cicero thought it was at Atticus' instigation (8. 5. 1). I fancy that in disclaiming any wish to have pressure brought to bear on Dionysius for the present, Cicero does not mean to preclude his friend from offering the man some gentle admonition which might bring him to a better frame of mind.

M and other MSS. have *si* for *nisi* in 2. 9. 2 and 12. 16. 1. For the converse error see on 8. 9a. 2 and 12. 37. 2 (p. 91).

7. 20. 1   breviloquentem iam me tempus ipsum facit. pacem enim desperavi, bellum nostri nullum administrant. cave enim putes quicquam esse minoris his consulibus. *quorum* ego spe audiendi aliquid et cognoscendi nostri apparatus maximo imbri Capuam veni.

'De structura cf. Madvig ad Cic., De fin., 1, 18, 60 *quarum potiendi spe*': Madvig's notes are not for editors who think that *quos sperans me auditurum aliquid* would be Latin, or who do not think at all.[1] '*quorum . . . aliquid* (i.e. *spe audiendi ex iis aliquid*) varie temptata; cfr. Madv. de fin. IV 13[32]': genitives like *haec Epicuri* or *quid simile Milonis* only prove that *quorum aliquid* could mean 'something in the consuls'. From the twentieth century turn to the sixteenth: 'quarum ego rerum spe audiendi aliquid' (Malaespina). The indefinite neuter *quorum*, with reference to the matters comprised in the sentence *pacem . . . administrant*, may be defended by the same use of *quae* (nom. and acc.) in e.g. 5. 20. 1 *quae cognosce*, 9. 11 A. 3 *quae si tantum*. As for the parenthesis *cave enim . . . consulibus*, there is no great rarity in finding as the antecedent of a relative pronoun, not the nearest grammatically possible noun, but something farther away, as in 8. 4. 1 *cui qui noster honos . . . defuit?*, Nep. *Dat.* 8. 3 *quibus fretus* (see also my note on Prop. 2. 26. 47). Here this makes for undeniable obscurity, and I am far from confident that the text is sound. But if it is to stand, there is no other way to prop it up.

7. 26. 2   quod addis, ne propensior ad turpem causam videar, *certe videri* possum. ego me ducem in civili bello, quoad de pace ageretur, n⟨eg⟩avi esse, non quin rectum esset, sed quia, quod multo rectius fuit, id mihi fraudem tulit.

videri edd. vett.: videre Ω

'Nullo modo Cicero se ad turpem causam propensiorem videri posse concedit, quaeque sequuntur, ad omnem huiusmodi reprehensionem removendam pertinent' (Madvig). Perhaps this is too emphatic, but there is certainly something odd about a flat admission, which can hardly be understood εἰρωνικῶς (Manutius). The old insertion of a negative is better than Madvig's *ridere*. Another possibility is *certe⟨n⟩ videri possum?*, 'can I really seem so?' For *certen* see *T.L.L.* III, 930. 63 ff. (the simple *certe* is so used by Augustus ap. Suet. *Aug.* 33. 1 *certe patrem tuum non occidisti?*, if the text is sound, and by Val. Fl. 7. 385). The rendering 'I allow that I may *seem* so' would be easier if we had *videri certe possum*; and that also is possible.

[1] For example TP, who do not see that this is implied.

BOOK VIII

8. 2. 4 significas enim...ut etiam Italia, si ille cedat, putes cedendum. quod ego nec rei p. puto esse utile nec liberis meis,
praeterea neque rectum neque honestum. *sed cur* 'poterisne
igitur videre tyrannum?' quasi intersit, audiam an videam *et sqq.*

sed cur, 'but why [do you ask]?' is not in logic demonstrably
wrong, but like many others I find it hard to believe that it is right.
sed tu (Purser) does not, I think, elsewhere introduce an imaginary
objection. Müller's *videtur*, taken with what precedes, is possible,
but *sequitur*, 'follows the question', would lead more easily to the
corruption (perhaps it was divided into *se q cur*). Cf. 15. 11. 3
sequebatur ut mecum ipse, Rab. Post. 29 '*moreretur*', *inquies; nam id
sequitur*. Having decided that neither expediency nor duty require
him to leave Italy, Cicero turns to face a different argument: can he
bear to watch a tyrant at close quarters?

8. 3. 5 vidi nihil quaeri praeter fugam. eam si nunc sequor,
quonam? cum illo non; ad quem cum essem profectus, cognovi
in iis locis esse Caesarem ut tuto Luceriam venire non possem.
infero mari nobis incerto cursu hieme maxima navigandum est.

   quonam (quo nam) *Mms*, quoniam *bdEOR*, qui *P*

No editor thinks *quanam* (Frederking[1]) worth recording. It is
clearly right, since the answer concerns route, not destination.

8. 5. 2 pendeo animi exspectatione Corfiniensi, *in* qua de salute rei
publicae decernetur.

   TP add *de re* before *Corfiniensi*, Otto *de obsidione*. The difficulty
does not lie in the expression *exspectatio Corfiniensis*; see Reid's note
in TP ad loc., and cf. such phrases as 14. 10. 1 *Capitolino die*, Fam.
3. 8. 9 *sententia bima*, Liv. 40. 12. 7 *nocturno argumento*, Quint. *Inst.*
12. 10. 4 *Peloponnesia tempora*. It lies in the statement 'that the
safety of the state depended on the expectation and not on the thing
expected'.[2] *Ad Brut.* 2. 2. 2 *nos exspectatio sollicitat, quae est omnis*

---

[1] *Philol.* 1899, p. 630. He also conjectured *quonam ⟨modo⟩*.
[2] TP, vol. VI, p. 116.

iam in extremum adducta discrimen is not parallel, even if the text is sound; suspense can reach a crisis. But Watt there marks a lacuna after *sollicitat*. The simplest remedy is to delete *in* (*i* was written twice). *qua* depends on *Corfinium*, understood from *Corfiniensi*: see Mayor on *N.D.* 1. 89 *quae* and cf. Sall. *Iug.* 66. 2 *Vagenses quo Metellus . . . praesidium imposuerat*, Just. 36. 2. 1 *Iudaeis origo Damascena, Syriae nobilissima civitas*, Eur. *Andr.* 652 οὖσαν μὲν Ἠπειρῶτιν, οὗ et sqq., *Hec.* 710 f. Θρήκιος ἱππότας, ἵνα et sqq.

8. 9a. 2 VI Kal. vesperi Balbus minor ad me venit occulta via
     currens ad Lentulum consulem missu Caesaris cum litteris,
     cum mandatis, cum promissione provinciae, Romam ut redeat.
     cui persuaderi posse non arbitror *nisi* erit conventus.

Manutius mentions a reading *nisi non erit* in a MS. belonging to a friend and hence proposes *posse arbitror nisi non erit conventus.* Lambinus follows him. Three centuries later Nipperdey[1] observed 'etwas zu leugnen außer für den fall, in welchem es allein möglich ist, ist nicht witzig, sondern abgeschmackt': hence *posse arbitror si erit conventus.* Editors pay little heed, or none. *si* for *nisi* is all that is needed: 'I don't think he can be persuaded, if Balbus succeeds in meeting him.' If Balbus did *not* meet him there would evidently be no question of his persuasions proving effective.

8. 11D. 4 qui regionibus exclusi intra praesidia atque intra arma
     aliena venissent.

The text needs explanation, not emendation. *regionibus* means 'by whole districts', i.e. large tracts of country: cf. Curt. 4. 2. 16 *exhauriendas esse regiones ut illud spatium exaggeraretur*, Ov. *Her.* 15. 125 *quamvis regionibus absis* (Palmer wrong, Purser right), *Met.* 12. 41. Wesenberg's *regionibus ⟨suis⟩* is quite wrong, though ⟨*a suis*⟩ ('from their own side') would make the sense plainer: cf. 8. 12B. 1 *priusquam Caesar . . . me abs te excludere posset.*

8. 11D. 7 memineram me esse unum qui pro meis maximis in rem
     p. meritis supplicia miserrima et crudelissima pertulissem, me
     esse unum qui, si offendissem eius animum cui tum, cum iam in
     armis essemus, consulatus tamen alter et triumphus amplissi-

[1] *Philol.* 1848, pp. 148 f.

mus deferebatur, subicerer eisdem proeliis, *ut* mea persona
semper ad improborum civium impetus aliquid videretur habere
populare.

This is a tortuous sentence in an uneasy letter, but, while recogniz-
ing the difficulty of *ut...videretur*, I do not think it necessary to
substitute *quod, et,* or *cum*. It may be explained thus: Cicero is very
apt to use *videri* in a consecutive clause when he wants to make a
comment for which he prefers not to take full responsibility: cf.
1. 19. 3 *hoc idem post me Pompeio accidit, ut nos duo quasi pignora rei
publicae retineri videremur*, *Clu.* 178 *unum, alterum, tertium annum
Sassia quiescebat, ut velle atque optare aliquid calamitatis filio potius
quam id struere et moliri videretur*, *Leg. Agr.* 2. 3 *(reperietis) me
esse unum ex omnibus novis hominibus...qui...consul factus sim
cum primum petierim, ut vester honos...non...diuturnis precibus
efflagitatus, sed dignitate impetratus esse videatur*, *Phil.* 14. 32 *vos
vero patriae natos iudico, quorum etiam nomen a Marte est, ut idem
deus urbem hanc gentibus, vos huic urbi genuisse videatur*, *De Or.*
1. 202 *non enim causidicum...conquirimus, sed eum virum qui sit eius
artis antistes cuius...auctor tamen esse deus putatur, ut id ipsum,
quod erat hominis proprium, non partum per nos, sed divinitus ad nos
delatum videretur*, 3. 10 *neque vero longe ab eo C. Iuli caput...iacuit,
ut ille, qui haec non vidit, et vixisse cum re publica pariter et cum illa
simul exstinctus esse videatur*.

This passage is exactly similar, except that he imagines himself to
be making the comment *ut...habere videretur* (i.e. *quasi haberet*) in
circumstances which might have arisen, but in fact have not. If they
had, he could have said *isdem proeliis obicior, ut...videatur*.

8. 12A. 1   quod veritus sum, factum est, ut Domitius implicaretur,
neque ipse satis firmus esset ad castra facienda...neque ⟨se⟩, si
vellet, expedire posset.

neque ipse *M^cbdmsEO²RP*: ut neque ipse *MO*   se *add. Lambinus*

The writer is Pompey.

neque...neque are obviously correlative. Sjögren may be right in
reading *ut* before the first *neque*, with the first hands of M and O.
Madvig's *et* may look more elegant, but the sequence of *ut* clauses,
the second depending on the first, is unobjectionable (cf. e.g. 13. 19. 5

ut non sim consecutus ut superior mea causa videatur). However most MSS. and editions have neither *ut* nor *et*. It is possible to do without them, but only if the first *neque* be allowed a dual function, correlating with *implicaretur* on the one hand and with the following *neque* on the other. This is an un-Ciceronian phenomenon, but not uncommon in historians (see Leumann–Hofmann, p. 663). It occurs in Caesar's letter 9. 6A *cum Furnium nostrum tantum vidissem, neque loqui neque audire meo commodo potuissem.*

8. 14. 1　Brundisii autem omne certamen vertitur huius *primi* temporis

'*huius primi temporis*] "of this first stage of the war"' (TP). But how was Cicero to know at the beginning of March 49 that the siege of Brundisium would not turn out to be the last stage? In relation to the battle for Italy it actually was the last, and I imagine that Cicero, if the point had occurred to him, would have distinguished two earlier stages—the first ending with the abandonment of the capital, the second with the surrender of Corfinium. For *primi* read *proximi* ('these next few days'). For the corruption see Housman on Man. 5. 218.

8. 16. 1　quomodo autem se venditant Caesari! municipia vero *ad eum*, nec simulant, ut cum de illo aegroto vota faciebant.

ad eum *M²bmsEORP*, ad deum *d*, deum *M* (d *deletum*, ad *superscriptum*)

The conjecture *ut deo* in TP's text is renounced in their apparatus in deference to Sjögren's defence of *ad eum* as equivalent to ἀπαντῶσι.[1] This sense is adequate, though scarcely happy as an anticipation of *quas fieri censes* ἀπαντήσεις *ex oppidis* below; and ellipse of *venire*, if not of *legatos mittere*, needs no defence. It is rather a question of style. Colour and emphasis are essential here; *ad eum* is bathos. *ad caelum* [sc. *ferunt*] would be colourful enough, and, though Cicero does not elsewhere suppress the verb in this phrase, such an ellipse in a stock expression like *ad* (*in*) *caelum ferre* (*efferre, tollere*) would not be surprising: cf. e.g. *operam* for *operam dedi* in 4. 15. 6. But on the whole I would return with Winstedt to *deum* [sc. *faciunt*]: cf. Ter. *Ad.* 535 *facio te apud illum deum.*

[1] Χάριτες F. Leo, pp. 260 f.

BOOK IX

9. 6. 2   Domitius, ut audio, in Cosano est, ⟨et⟩ quidem, ut aiunt, paratus ad navigandum; si in Hispaniam non *probo*, si ad Cn., laudo.

Why does Cicero disapprove of Domitius' going to Spain? Reasons are imaginable no doubt, but the context does nothing to suggest them. *non ⟨im⟩probo* would give a clear point and accord much better with Cicero's known sentiments. For Domitius to go to Spain would be neither very laudable nor blameworthy, but if he joined Pompey after Pompey's desertion of him at Corfinium, that would be magnanimity.

9. 6. 7   melioris medius fidius civis et viri putabam quovis supplicio adfici quam illi crudelitati non solum praeesse verum etiam interesse. videtur vel mori satius fuisse quam esse cum his.

Schütz thought *videtur...cum his* a gloss. These words are indeed, as they stand, an insufferably feeble reiteration of the preceding statement that anything would be better than participation in Pompey's war plans, not to be salved by quibbles.[1] But *his*, as Orelli perceived, suggests the Caesarians: cf. 9. 7. 5 *horum insanias*, ibid. *nec tam ut illa adiuvem quam ut haec ne videam cupio discedere*, 9. 11. 4 *sed certe et haec perdita sunt et illa non salutaria*. I suggest that *sed* has fallen out after *interesse*. It is Cicero's usual dilemma: to take a hand in Pompeian cruelties would be bad, but to stay among the Caesarians is no better.

9. 7. 6   bonis viris quod ais probari quae adhuc fecerimus, scirique ab iis non profectos, valde gaudeo, si est nunc ullus gaudendi locus.

profectos *PZ*[b] *cod. Faerni*: profectis *Δ* (prae- *bd*) *OR*

Preoccupied by the omission of *nos* after *sciri*, which is no doubt defensible, editors omit to ask *why* it should please Cicero to know that the *boni* were aware of his failure to join Pompey. Their knowledge of it might surely have been taken for granted; what he wanted

---

[1] As Boot's 'in *supplicio* non opus est mortem cogitare'.

to hear was that they did not judge it harshly. Something has fallen out; perhaps *non ⟨sine causa non⟩ profectos*[1] (cf. 9. 9. 4 *nec sine causa...times*).

9. 10. 6   deinde III Id. Febr. iterum mihi respondes consulenti sic: 'quod quaeris a me *fugamne fidam an moram defendam* utiliorem putem, ego vero in praesentia subitum discessum et praecipitem profectionem cum tibi tum ipsi Cn. inutilem et periculosam puto et satius esse existimo vos dispertitos et in speculis esse; sed medius fidius turpe nobis puto esse de fuga cogitare.'

fidam] fedam *fort.* M, fidem *b*   deserendam *M*c(?)*msO*²

fugamne foedam an moram nefandam is the best answer here. *foedam* and *nefandam* are both old corrections, nowadays generally considered unworthy of mention in an apparatus criticus; for editors, instructed by Otto,[2] imagine that such epithets beg the question which Atticus has been asked to decide. Not at all. The alternatives, to flee from Italy or to stay, are both repugnant, flight being ignominious and staying impious (because it means deserting Pompey and what Cicero always at bottom feels to be the cause of the Republic). Setting these two evils before Atticus for choice, Cicero had asked him, not indeed which was the lesser, but, not without irony, which was the more expedient. An unfavourable epithet for either course is what his perplexity requires: cf. 7. 18. 1 *utrum turpi pace nobis an misero bello esset utendum.* Most modern texts receive Otto's *fugamne defendam an moram utiliorem putem*, one of the worst of many guesses.

The words must have been taken by Atticus from a lost letter, perhaps of February 6 or 7.

9. 10. 7   multa disputas huic sententiae convenientia; inde ad extremum: '"quid si", inquis, "Lepidus et Volcacius discedunt?" plane ἀπορῶ. quod evenerit igitur et quod egeris, id στερκτέον putabo.'

---

[1] ⟨*ratione*⟩ *non profectos* would be mechanically less attractive, but possibly more elegant writing; cf. 12. 44. 3 *quod domi te inclusisti, ratione fecisti.*

[2] *Rhein. Mus.* 1886, p. 371: 'All die zahlreichen Konjekturen...leiden an dem Grundfehler, daß sie das Urtheil Ciceros schon vorwegnehmen, während er sich doch erst bei seinem Freunde Atticus hatte Rath holen wollen.'

Editors print this as though *inquis* was Cicero's, accompanying the quotation from Atticus' letter. I doubt if *inquis* ever introduces an actual quotation in the Letters; it certainly does not in any of the other thirteen quotations from Atticus' side of the correspondence contained in §§4–9. It does, of course, commonly introduce an imaginary interlocution, as in 7. 5. 5 '*quid senties igitur?*', *inquis*. So here '*quid si*', *inquis*, ' . . . *discedunt*' in Atticus' letter is an imaginary question from Cicero, i.e. *inquis* is copied from that letter.

A similar phenomenon has caused confusion in 10. 4. 9 '*cupivi*', *inquit* [*Curio*], '*ex s.c. surrupto; nam aliter ⟨non⟩ poterat. at ille* [*Caesar*] *impendio nunc magis odit senatum. "a me", inquit, "omnia proficiscentur."*' Müller and TP correctly make Curio quote Caesar. Boot gives *at ille* et sqq. to Cicero. Others, as Orelli and Sjögren,[1] make Curio the subject of the second *inquit*, the latter[2] introducing the superfluous *ad senatum* from many MSS. into his text.

9. 11. 4   tuas litteras iam desidero. post fugam nostram numquam *iam nostrum* earum intervallum fuit.

      nostrum earum (eorum *R*) *ΔOR*, nostrum *E*, nostrarum *P*

The conjectures best worth attention are *tam longum earum* (Corradus; *tam vastum earum* Haupt) and *iam tantum earum* (Muretus), both of which find a place in modern texts. Müller pointed out that *nostrum* may be due entirely to the preceding *nostram*. No one, on the other hand, has to my knowledge drawn attention to the similarity in minuscule between *tantum* and *i$\bar{a}$ nrum* and wished to read *numquam tantum*.

9. 13. 3   quae si maxime meminissem, tamen illius temporis similitudinem iam sequi deberem. nihil me adiuvit, cum posset; at postea fuit amicus, etiam valde, nec quam ob causam plane scio. ergo ego quoque illi. quin etiam illud par in utroque nostrum, quod ab eisdem illecti sumus. sed utinam tantum ego ei prodesse potuissem quantum mihi ille potuit. mihi tamen quod fecit gratissimum. nec ego nunc eum iuvare qua re possim scio *et sqq.*

---

[1] *Symbolae Philologicae O. A. Danielsson* (1932), p. 323.

[2] With Moricca in tow. The Budé edition at present stops at 6. 8.

et postea *Ω, corr. Tyrrell–Purser*   et tam (quam *P*) ob causam *Ω, corr.*
Madvig   illecti sumus *Lambinus*: illectissimus *M*, lecti sumus *PZ¹*, dilecti
sumus *M²bdmsRO*   utinam tantum *Ω, corr. edd. vett.*

All is now well here. But if *utinam tantum...potuit* meant 'But
oh, that it had been in my power to render him as important a
service, as he was able to render me!' (Shuckburgh), it would be
otherwise. Then indeed *mihi tamen quod fecit gratissimum* 'would
seem to stand more appositely after *nec ego...putarem*' (TP). But
potuit does not refer to the service which Pompey actually rendered
in connection with Cicero's restoration from exile. It means 'had the
power to render', 'might have rendered', and should be understood
of the situation in 58, when Cicero, left in the lurch by the Optimates, turned to Pompey for aid which he did *not* get. All the same
(*tamen*. Not 'though I can do so little to show it'), he is grateful for
what Pompey did do later on, in 57.

9. 13. 5   sed habebam in illis et occultationem et ὑπηρεσίαν
  fidelem. quae si mihi Brundisii *suppetant*, mallem; sed ibi
  occultatio nulla est.

  suppeditant *O*

Ernesti's *suppeterent* remains in texts which have no place for
Wesenberg's *velit* in 11. 24. 2 *equidem tibi potissimum velim, si idem
illa vellet*. Such variations of tense are common in comedy. How far
they should be admitted into classical prose is doubtful,[1] but to substitute a palaeographically none too plausible[2] conjecture in a familiar
letter is unnecessarily despotic.

9. 18. 3   'vidisti igitur virum, ut scripseras? ingemuisti?' certe.
  'cedo reliqua.' quid? continuo ipse in Pedanum, ego Arpinum;
  inde expecto quidem λαλαγεῦσαν illam tuam. 'tu malim',
  inquies, 'actum ne agas. etiam illum ipsum quem sequimur
  multa fefellerunt.'

  malim *Boot*: malum *M*, malem *RP*, mallem *M²bdmsO*

So, according to the usual distribution of the words, ends Cicero's
account of his interview with Caesar on 28 March 49. Apart from

[1] See Kühner–Stegmann, II, p. 401.
[2] Neither the addition of *er* nor the change of vowel is separately difficult,
but I have not noticed both corruptions combined elsewhere in these MSS.

Pedanum, which I do not here discuss, the difficulties are not sufficiently appreciated by commentators. Here is TP's rendering:

You will say, *Have you seen the man then to be as you have written of him*
(headstrong and self-willed) *? and did you heave a sigh?* Indeed I did. *Tell
me the rest*, you say. What more is there to tell? He is going to Pedum, I to
Arpinum. After that I wait for your swallow. [You will say] *I would
rather not have you crying over spilt milk; even our leader Pomepy has often
gone wrong.*

(*a*) *vidisti igitur virum* [sc. *esse*] *ut scripseras?* is doubtful in point
of Latinity. TP compare 7. 2. 3 *adulescentem ut nosti* (q.v.), but there
too the text has been suspected. On the whole I incline to think it
admissible, but if the question is supposed to come from Atticus then
this interpretation (an old one) clashes with § 1 *illa fefellerunt, facilem
quod putaramus*. Cicero at least, and probably both Cicero and
Atticus (*putaramus*), had thought Caesar would take an accommo-
dating line at the interview; he cannot have written that Caesar
would be headstrong and self-willed. Two other explanations have
been proposed. (i) *virum* is emphasized, as opposed to *hominem*:
'ut Atticus id verbum usurpet, quo Cicero in epistola quadam usus
erat, cum scriberet fortasse sic: *Ego cum virum videro*; ἐμφατικῶς de
Caesare' (Manutius). But what has Caesar's manliness to do with
the case? (ii) 'So you've seen him then, as you wrote that you would?'
This is the natural meaning of the words apart from their context;
but why make Atticus ask such a question, and why make him add
ut scripseras? There can be no implication of surprise, as in 5. 2. 2
'*non vidisti igitur hominem?*' *inquies*. It was on Atticus' advice that
Cicero decided to face Caesar at Formiae, as long ago as the 11th
(9. 6. 1), and in the intervening letters there is never a doubt but
that he would do so: cf., for example, 9. 15. 1 *eum cum videro Arpinum
pergam*.

None of these interpretations is helped by the removal of the
question-mark after *scripseras*.

(*b*) Why should Atticus want to be told that Cicero groaned?
And when did he groan? Not during the interview, presumably.
The idea of his groaning after it was over is odd to my mind, especially
as he was very well satisfied with his own part in it (§ 1 *ita discessi-
mus. credo igitur hunc me non amare. at ego me amavi, quod mihi iam
pridem usu non venit*). *ingemiscere* occurs seven times elsewhere in

the Letters, always of an immediate reaction to some thought, or piece of news, or event. In three of these cases Cicero pictures his correspondent groaning at something in his own letter: 1. 1. 1 *puto te in hoc aut risisse aut ingemuisse*, 7. 23. 1 *et non omnes nostra corpora opponimus? in quo tu quoque ingemiscis*, Q. *Fr.* 2. 9 (8). 2 *verebor ne quando ego tibi, cum sum una, molestus sim. video te ingemuisse.*

Here, surely, he does the same. The words *vidisti...certe* are Cicero's, not (in Cicero's imagination) Atticus'. Thus: *vidisti igitur virum ut scripseras? ingemuisti certe. 'cedo reliqua.'* 'Have you seen here the man as your letter had pictured him? I am sure you groaned [as you read].' The question, thus rendered, is ironical. Atticus may well be supposed to have written something comfortable, as that, having reached a satisfactory adjustment with Caesar, which would not be difficult, Cicero would be able to await the 'spring swallow' (i.e. the time to leave Italy) without anxiety about the interval. It had turned out far otherwise, and Cicero does not refrain from reminding him of his mistake both by the question and by the repetition of his phrase about the swallow. Atticus' *actum ne agas* (which must in any case refer to the error as to Caesar's attitude alluded to in § 1) then gains much in relevance and point. 'Don't keep harping on past mistakes. After all I am not the only man in the world whose predictions have gone astray.'

This is to take *ut scripseras* as TP do, and is open to the same linguistic objection. There is another possibility: 'Have you then seen the man, as you put it?' Atticus may have urged him to send a detailed and graphic account, so that he could 'see' Caesar as he read. *certe* will then mean 'at any rate'. It is one of many cases where doubt could only be removed by the resurrection of the other side of the correspondence.

As for *malum*, an impatient explanation 'Confound it!' would be quite appropriate, and the prohibition *ne agas* is defensible in a proverbial expression. Boot's point[1] that Cicero always follows this interjection with *iste* except in *Rosc. Com.* 56 (where he would introduce it) is far from conclusive. The real objection has not, I think, been raised—that exclamatory *malum* is only found in questions.

[1] *Mnemos.* 1890, pp. 356 f.

BOOK X

10. 1. 1   per enim magni aestimo tibi firmitudinem animi nostri et factum nostrum probari. Sexto *enim* nostro quod scribis probari, ita laetor ut me quasi patris eius...iudicio me comprobari putem.

If the second *enim* is right the meaning must be as TP incline to take it '[I will not say I merely value], for I am delighted with the approval of Peducaeus'. *nam* is often used in this elliptical fashion, *enim* rarely, if ever. The preceding *enim* reinforces a suspicion of corruption. E offers *enim* for *quidem* in 9. 2a. 2 and for *cui* in 9. 5. 2, a contiguous *enim* being to blame in both places. In 8. 14. 3 the second *enim* is by common consent replaced with Madvig's *etiam*. Schütz's *etiam* (or *autem*) is probably right in 16. 1. 5 *videndum enim est* (with *enim* before and after). Either *etiam* or, as Professor Watt suggests, *autem* might be read here.

10. 1. 3   sed tamen hominis hoc ipsum probi est *et magnum sit* ⟨τ⟩ῶν πολιτικωτάτων σκεμμάτων, veniendumne sit in consilium tyranni si is aliqua de re bona deliberaturus sit.

et *om. Δ*   σκεμμάτων *C*: cκεματα *M*, cτικεματα (cπκ-) *RP*, σκέμματα *M^cbdms*

Many critics have fumbled with this passage, and most editors obelize. Not so Sjögren, content to replace *sit ων* by *est τῶν* and with *probi est* to understand σκέψασθαι. Two points seem to me sufficiently clear:

First, *sed tamen...probi est* is a question. Cicero is discussing the idea that he might be asked by Caesar to undertake peace negotiations. He himself sees no prospect of peace, because Caesar is determined upon Pompey's destruction. Possibly, indeed, Caesar might allow a quiet interval for envoys to pass to and fro, but there was no real hope. Anyhow (*sed tamen*), apart from the hopelessness of result, could a good citizen act as Caesar's negotiator at all?

Secondly, σκεμμάτων is a partitive genitive of a kind common in Greek.

Cicero's *meaning* is plain. 'It is a great question (σκέμμα magnum, cf. 7. 21. 3), and one of the highest relevance to statesmen (cf. 7. 8. 3 *est πολιτικὸν σκέμμα*), whether', etc. This might have been expressed *magna est quaestio et ex maxime civilibus*; with the Greek genitive it might have been *magnum est σκέμμα et τῶν πολιτικωτάτων*. As we have it *σκέμμα* is attracted by a bold metathesis into the case of *πολιτικωτάτων*.

The following will at least approximate to what Cicero wrote: *sed tamen hominis hoc ipsum probi est? et magnum est et*[1] *τῶν πολιτικωτάτων σκεμμάτων*[2] *et sqq.*

10. 4. 11   iurabat ad summam, quod nullo negotio *faceret*, amicissimum mihi Caesarem esse debere.

All modern editors discredit *faceret*, nearly all in favour of *facere solet* (Orelli). I submit that *quod nullo negotio* [=*facile*] *faceret* may stand as legitimate, if idiomatic, Latin for 'as he could easily do'.[3] An oath cost Curio nothing, but whether he spoke the truth was another matter. For *facile* with the potential subjunctive cf., for example, 2. 22. 6 *quod facile sentias*, *Fam.* 1. 7. 3 *quod facile intellexerim*, Curt. 8. 2. 35 *quod facile appareret*. If the reference had been to the future Cicero might have written *iurabit, quod nullo negotio faciat*, probably without censure.

10. 8. 2   relinquitur ut, si vincimur in Hispania, quiescamus. id
ego contra puto. istum enim victorem magis relinquendum
puto quam victum, et dubitantem magis quam fidentem suis
rebus.

'Schütz and others have altered *et* to *nec*, an easy but unnecessary proceeding' (TP). An easier still is to translate words which Lambinus did not understand like this: 'For I think I am more bound to turn my back on Caesar as victor, rather than when he is conquered and is in a critical, rather than a confident, state as regards his fortunes.' Easiest of all to print the vulgate without hint of difficulty or conjecture. Less easy to follow Cicero's meaning, which, so

---

[1] *est magnum sittybum et* O. E. Schmidt.
[2] *σκέμμα* Orelli, perhaps rightly.
[3] Cf. 'as well he might'.

far as I know, only A. Frederking has done.[1] Cicero disagrees with
the opinion that he should lie low in Italy if Caesar wins in Spain
because Caesar victorious will be worse than Caesar defeated; and,
this much granted, it follows that it is better to leave *now*, while
Caesar is still doubtful of success, than later, when he will be confident of it. For, as the next sentence explains, once Caesar wins,
massacre and confiscation will be the order of the day. The words
et . . . suis rebus are relevant, not indeed to the hypothetical problem
of what to do if Caesar wins, but to the actual problem which is
the main theme of this letter, namely, whether to await the outcome
in Spain before taking action.

10. 10. 2   *tuum consilium quam verum est.* nam qui se medium esse
vult, in patria manet, qui proficiscitur, aliquid de altera utra
parte iudicare videtur.

quam M^2bdmsO^2: quia Md^2ORP

Thus begins Antony's reply to letters summarized in §1. These
were to the effect that Cicero had no intentions adverse to Caesar,
but desired to go abroad to escape the embarrassment of moving
about in Italy with his lictors; though even yet he had not definitely
made up his mind to this (*nec id ipsum certum etiam nunc habere*).

The first sentence must be unsound, as Madvig saw.[2] Whether
quam is exclamatory or the equivalent of *perquam*,[3] the words can
only be understood as an emphatic endorsement of Cicero's 'plan'.
In explanation (*nam*) follows a sound and obvious reason for dis-
approving it: departure from Italy would be an unneutral act. The
contradiction has not passed unobserved, and commentators are
reduced to asserting that *quam verum* is ironic or that *consilium*
means, not the plan to go abroad to which all the rest of Antony's
note refers, but the slight amount of hesitation conveyed by *nec id
ipsum certum etiam nunc habere*. The latter view refutes itself. As for
the former, it is unimaginable that Antony should begin a letter to
the famous consular, for whom he and his master professed affection

[1] In the main. His note in *Philol.* 1900, pp. 155 f., is rather meagre and not free
from secondary error. Winstedt's translation also, though unsatisfactory, may
be based on understanding.
[2] *Adv. Crit.* III, p. 186, n.
[3] Unlikely. Antony would hardly have used such a colloquialism to Cicero.

and respect (cf. 10. 8A), with a piece of insulting, heavy-handed sarcasm.

The archetype evidently had *quia*, which does not seem to help. If *verum consilium* is rightly interpreted here as 'a sound plan' something may have fallen out, e.g. *tuum consilium quam verum sit ⟨nescio⟩.* Otherwise *tuorum* might replace *tuum*, since Cicero could well have mentioned that his Caesarian friends, such as Dolabella and Caelius (cf. 10. 9A, just received) had counselled him to stay in Italy. This gives *consilium verum* its normal sense, 'sound' (or 'honest') 'advice': so in the passages quoted in *T.L.L.* IV, 455. 29–31 and in others there omitted (9. 7A. 1, *Q. Fr.* 3. 1. 20, *Amic.* 44, [Sall.] *Ep. ad Caes.* 2. 10. 3, 2. 12. 2). But on the other hand there is 4. 5. 1 *recta, vera, honesta consilia.*

10. 12. 3   Q. f. severius adhibebo. utinam proficere *possem*!

posse (?) *W*

Pius' conjecture *possim* is generally read. The change is of the easiest, but I do not think it an improvement. The imperfect implies hopelessness of result, quite appropriate here. So in *Fam.* 15. 21. 3 *cui quidem ego amori utinam ceteris rebus possem! amore certe respondebo,* and often.

10. 12a. 4   nos iuveni, ut rogas, suppeditabimus et Peloponnesum
    ipsam sustinebimus. est enim indoles, modo aliquod *hoc sit*
ἦθος ΑΚΙΜΟΛΟΝ

aliquid *msRP*   ακιμολον (-αον *Mm*) *MmOW*(?)*Z^β*, ΑΚΙ ΑΛΛΟΛΟΝ*Z^b*, ΑΚΙΚΤΟΝΜΟΑΟΝ *R*, ακηκτοημολον *P*

huic sit or *in hoc sit* is useless patchwork, for the demonstrative is superabundant if referred to *iuveni* (i.e. *Quinto filio*). Perhaps *huic adsit,* 'if only this might be supported by...'. For the Greek there are many guesses; mine is ἦθος ἄκακον καὶ ἄδολον.[1] 'Parablepsy' from ΚΑ to ΚΑ produces ΑΚΑΙΑΔΟΛΟΝ, which is very close to *Z^b*. This was Cicero's fixed opinion of his nephew: 6. 2. 2 *sed est magnum illud quidem, verum tamen multiplex pueri ingenium,* 10. 6. 2 *mirabilia multa, nihil simplex, nihil sincerum.*

[1] κακίᾳ ἄδολον Gronovius ap. Orelli.

BOOK XI

11. 5. 4　quod de Vatinio quaeris, neque illius neque cuiusquam mihi praeterea officium *deest*, si reperire possent qua in re me iuvarent.

Most editors read *de(e)sset*, and even Sjögren hesitates. I think the indicative may stand: 'they are ready to help, (and would help) if only they could'. Cf. Tac. *Ann.* 1. 19. 3 *si tenderent...cur meditentur* with Furneaux' note, Liv. 9. 23. 10 *et, si homines iuvare velint, iniqua loca sunt* (sim. Plaut. *Amph.* 336, *Stich.* 27 f.), Mart. 2. 63. 3 *luxuria est, si tanti dives amares. deesset* would not quite express what Cicero wants to say, that these people actually are doing all they can.

11. 6. 2　(27 Nov. 48)　quos [*sc.* lictores] ego *non* paulisper cum bacillis in turbam conieci ad oppidum accedens, ne quis impetus militum fieret.

non can hardly be right. The emphasis it lays on the duration of the incident is pointless. Boot and others have *nunc* (Tunstall), 'satis absurde' as Risberg says.[1] His conjecture *vero*, in fact an old reading, is not much better, nor is there any plausibility in Gurlitt's[2] *Non.* or TP's *tamen. non* may be deleted (Lehmann), or replaced by *modo* (another early reading, proposed afresh by Reid), or again by *nuper*; for if *per* (*p*) fell out before *p*, *nu* would easily become $\overline{no}$. Cicero reached Brundisium from Greece about the middle of October.

11. 7. 1　gratae tuae mihi litterae sunt, quibus accurate perscripsisti omnia quae ad me pertinere arbitratus es. *et factum igitur tu scribis istis placere ⟨et placere⟩ isdem istis lictoribus me uti, quod concessum Sestio sit.*

es. et *Sternkopf*: est ea *Md*, es. tea *m*, es ea *R*, es. eo *P* (?), est ita *O*, es *bs*
tu *Sternkopf*: ut *Ω* et placere *add. Sternkopf*

So modern editors, but assuredly not so Cicero, who may have written ...*arbitratus es. ita faciam igitur ut scribis istis placere,*

[1] *Eranos*, 1915, p. 179.
[2] *Philol.* 1920, pp. 300–6.

isdem et sqq. *faciam* is Madvig's, but his supplements are needless. 'I shall do therefore as you say they advise, i.e. that I should go on using these same lictors.'

11. 8. 2   *Furnius* est illic, mihi inimicissimus.

This name can scarcely be right. As has often been pointed out, C. Furnius was Cicero's constant friend both before and after December 48. TP are correct in rejecting *Fufius* (Calenus), who was in Achaea, not Alexandria (*illic*). Their suggestion *Furius* (Crassipes) is certainly tenable, but, though it is true that Cicero's relations with his former son-in-law do not seem to have been very cordial, Crassipes' visit to Formiae in March 49 (9. 11. 3) does not suggest bitter enmity. Moreover, Cicero elsewhere calls him by his cognomen. The only other similar name I can think of as suitable is Fulvius. *Att.* 4. 18. 3 of October 54 mentions the condemnation of a M. Fulvius Nobilior, who was probably the Catilinarian knight of Sall. *Cat.* 17. 4 (see *RE*, *Fulvius*, no. 94). Two things can fairly be assumed about him: that he was an enemy of Cicero's, and that, if alive, he was recalled from exile by Caesar in 49.

11. 9. 1   ego vero et incaute, ut scribis, et celerius quam oportuit feci, nec in ulla sum spe, quippe qui exceptionibus edictorum retinear. quae si non essent sedulitate effectae et benevolentia *tua*, liceret mihi abire in solitudines aliquas.

benivolentia tua $M^2bdmsEORP$: benivolentie ua M, benivolentiae qua W

Apart from the evidence of M and W, *tua* is unlikely. If Atticus had been individually responsible for getting Cicero's name into Antony's edict we should probably have heard more of it. Sternkopf's rather wild guess *Va⟨tini⟩* finds an unexpected home in Sjögren's text. Purser's *prava* is hardly better. *vestra* (*ura̅*) might be considered.[1] Influential well-wishers like Balbus and Oppius as well as Atticus would naturally have helped in this matter. So. 3. 24, from exile, begins *antea, cum ad me scripsissetis vestro consensu* et sqq.

[1] Perhaps, in view of W *effectae* [*et*] *benevolentiaque vestra* (*-q; ura̅*).

11. 15. 1 ille enim ita videtur *Alexandriam tenere* ut eum scribere etiam pudeat de illis rebus.

This is translatable: 'he seems to hold Alexandria, but on such terms that. . .'. Two minimal changes restore what I believe Cicero wrote, *Alexandria teneri*, 'is stuck in Alexandria': cf. 5. 20. 3 *Cassio qui Antiochia tenetur*, Ov. *Ex P*. 1. 3. 65 *Smyrna virum tenuit, non Pontus et hostica tellus*. Caesar was besieged at the time, hence Schütz's *illum. . . Alexandria*.

11. 24. 2 sed ad meam manum redeo; erunt enim haec occultius
agenda. vide, quaeso, etiam nunc de testamento, quod tum
factum cum illa quaerere coeperat. non, credo, te commovit;
neque enim rogavit ne me quidem. sed quasi ita sit, quoniam in
sermonem iam venisti, poteris eam monere ut alicui committat
cuius extra periculum huius belli fortuna sit. equidem tibi
potissimum velim, si idem illa vellet. quam quidem celo
miseram me hoc timere.

quaerere *edd. vett.*: querere *Ω*   et commoti (-os *O²*) neque eum rogari
Ω, corr. Gronovius   sermonem *bs*: sermone *cett.*   aliquoi *Mm²s*, aliqua
Mᶜdm   fortunas te quidem *Ω, corr. Manutius*

So Sjögren. I would add *vellem* after *factum* and (Lambinus) a comma after *rogavit*, and render as follows: 'Please see to the matter of the will even at this stage. I wish that had been done when she [Terentia] began to make enquiries. I imagine she didn't distress you; for, after all, she made no request of you, nor of me either. But as though it were so [i.e. as though you were concerned about it], now that the subject has been broached between you, you will be able to advise her. . . .'

It is impossible to unravel the whole story. This letter was written on 6 August 47, after several earlier mentions of the topic of Terentia's will. The first is 11. 16. 5 (3 June): *extremum est, quod te orem, si putas rectum esse et a te suscipi posse, cum Camillo communices, ut Terentiam moneatis de testamento. tempora monent ut videat ut satis faciat quibus debeat. auditum ex Philotimo est eam scelerate quaedam facere. credibile vix est, sed certe, si quid est quod fieri possit, providendum est.* 11. 25. 3 of 5 July is hopelessly corrupt, and 11. 23. 1 of 9 July unhelpful. It would seem that Cicero was anxious lest Terentia should somehow deal unfairly with their children, especially Tullia, in this will. She had consulted Atticus on some point, exactly what we cannot know, but it may have related to the possible confiscation of her property. Atticus had not felt much concern, since he was not asked to do anything. Cicero now suggests to him that, since the ice has been broken, he can recommend her to put the will[1] in the custody of some other person, such as Atticus himself, whose property is in no danger. 11. 16. 5 indicates his real motive—to forestall any 'criminal' move on Terentia's part.

BOOK XII

12. 2   I wish to leave questions of date for future study. But it is not too soon to contradict the stultifying ascription of this letter to 4 or 5 May 46, in which recent editors have followed Schiche. It must have been written, as used to be thought, before the arrival, about 20 April, of the news of Thapsus. *res interea fortasse transacta est* in §2 is not the only reason for concluding so, but it is reason enough—these words cannot tolerably be referred to mopping up operations. There are also the rumours of Caesarian misfortunes in §1; these are not the kind of reports which would have followed Caesar's decisive victory. When Cicero wrote 12. 4, placed in the modern arrangement before 12. 2, Cato's death was known; why then should rumour talk of fifty Caesarian ships carried off course to Utica, as though Utica was not already in Caesar's hands? §2 is nonsense if written in May. What could be less extraordinary (*o miros homines*) than Caesarians revelling *after* news of Caesar's triumph? Why should Balbus *not* build?[2]

12. 5   quod autem os in hanc rem ἔρανον a te! fac non ad διψῶσαν κρήνην, sed ad Πειρήνην eum venisse, ἄμπνευμα σεμνὸν

---

[1] *testamentum* is naturally taken to be the implied object of *committat*. Yet how could mere custody of the will by Atticus or another be any protection in the event of a confiscation? I suspect that a transfer of property was involved, but the details must remain obscure to unauthorized readers.

[2] Cicero's comment on that, *homini non recta sed voluptaria quaerenti nonne* βεβίωται? has sorely puzzled TP and their like. Manutius explains it.

'Αλφειοῦ, INTEPHNHN, ut scribis, *haurire*, in tantis suis praesertim angustiis.

INTEPHNHN *Mm, sim. O, om. RP*

Müller and Sjögren have *in te κρήνη* (Lehmann), and many add *et* (Malaespina) after *venisse*; but this is nothing. Read *hauriret*. Atticus had written that Quintus senior's demands would soon drain a διψῶσα κρήνη like himself. For *haurire* thus cf. *T.L.L.* VI, 2569. 10–17, Front. *Aq.* 9. 6 *Iuliam...quam hauriebant largiendo compendii sui gratia.* Cicero comments 'never mind a διψῶσα κρήνη, even Pirene couldn't satisfy Quintus'. Reconstruction of INTE-PHNHN can hardly be certain. Perhaps τὴν κρήνην.

12. 5b (June 45)   et vide, quaeso, L. Libo, ille qui de Ser. Galba, Censorinone et Manilio an T. Quintio, M' Acilio cos. tribunus pl. fuerit. conturbat enim me epitome Bruti Fanniana. *in Bruti epitome Fannianorum scripsi* quod erat in extremo, idque ego secutus hunc Fannium, qui scripsit historiam, generum esse scripseram Laelii. sed tu me γεωμετρικῶς refelleras, te autem nunc Brutus et Fannius. ego tamen de bono auctore, Hortensio, sic acceperam, ut apud Brutum est. hunc igitur locum expedies.

conturbat *CZ*[b]: conturbo Ω   epitome (Fannianorum)] epit(h)oma Ω
(epytonia *R*)

This puzzle seems insoluble. My purpose is to show, against editors who appeal to Münzer and Kurfess in their apparatus instead of obelizing their text, that it has not been solved. This requires a consideration of Münzer's lengthy, and in some ways helpful, article in *Hermes*,[1] along with A. Kurfess' supplementary note in the same periodical.[2] The only previous challenge to Münzer's main conclusions, and that on one point alone, comes from P. Fraccaro.[3]

Münzer's views may be summarized in two parts, as they concern (*a*) the historical problem of the two Fannii and (*b*) the interpretation of Cicero's text.

Contrary to Mommsen, he holds that the existence of two C. Fannii in the second half of the second century B.C. (Cic. *Brut.* 99

[1] 1920, pp. 427–42.   [2] 1922, pp. 623–5.
[3] *Athenaeum*, 1926, pp. 153–60.

horum aetatibus adiuncti duo C. Fannii C. et M. filii fuerunt) is firmly
established by the evidence set out in his article in *RE*.[1] He accepts
Cicero's statement (*Brut.* loc. cit.) that one was the son of a Marcus,
the other of a Gaius—this has since been confirmed by an inscrip-
tion discovered in Crete, which reveals a C. Fannius C. f. as one of a
senatorial commission (probably a praetorius) in 113.[2] But whereas
Cicero in the *Brutus* distinguishes between C. Fannius C. f., who
was consul in 122 and as tribune acted *arbitrio et auctoritate P.
Africani*, and C. Fannius M. f., historian and son-in-law of Laelius,
Münzer maintains that all these particulars apply to the son of
Marcus. For there is no doubt that the consul and tribune was
Marci filius,[3] and Cicero himself knew this when he wrote *Att.*
16. 13 c. 2 (November 44): *in praesentia mihi velim scribas quibus cos.
C. Fannius M. f. tr. pl. fuerit.* About the same time Cicero describes
the son-in-law of Laelius as *C. Fannio, Marci filio* (*Amic.* 3). So far
Münzer's guidance is demonstrably safe. For his identification of
the historian with this Marci filius there is no evidence beyond *Att.*
12. 5 b, and this is the point contested by Fraccaro.

As an interpreter Münzer is less successful than in his handling of
the historical evidence, and evasion of awkward but essential details
makes his exposition very hard to follow. However, he is right in
his first important contention, that the word *enim* points 'mit
zwingender Notwendigkeit' to what precedes, i.e. to the matter of
Libo's tribunate. With that the identity of Fannius has nothing to do.
So merely to expel *epitome Bruti Fanniana* or *in Bruti epitome
Fannianorum* from the text, as editors had generally done, leaves a
choice between changing *enim* to *etiam* with Orelli, Wesenberg, and
Boot and translating it 'too' with TP; and the former alternative is
over like tampering with a clue. Accordingly, *conturbat enim me
epitome Bruti Fanniana* is to be referred to the foregoing sentence,
not to the ensuing and unrelated topic of Fannius.

Here now is Münzer's final summary[4] of what he supposes to
have happened between Cicero and Atticus on this point. In the
Brutus Cicero had distributed four facts of biography between two
C. Fannii. Atticus refuted him mathematically by demonstrating

---

[1] VI. 2, 1987–90.
[2] Broughton, *Magistrates of the Roman Republic*, vol. I, p. 519, n. 2.
[3] Ibid.   [4] Loc. cit. p. 442.

from the Fasti that the tribune and consul was C. Fannius M. f., not
C. f. Cicero continued to believe in the distinction between the
persons, supposing only that the praenomina of the fathers had been
interchanged, and therefore that the history was the work of C.
Fannius C. f. Then, in Brutus' epitome of Fannius' history, he found
that the historian was described as M. f. So he turned for help to
Atticus, who explained the apparent contradiction by showing that
all four facts applied to one man.

This is none too clear. What, to start with, was the evidence on
which Cicero says he relied (*idque ego secutus*) for his identification
of Laelius' son-in-law with the historian? Münzer's answer is to be
gathered from his remarks on *scripsi*.[1] This word he reluctantly
gives up: 'Zu erwarten wäre ein *legi, vidi, quaesivi, repperi*[2] oder ein
sinnverwandter Ausdruck'—*scripsi* will have come from a copyist
whose eye strayed to *scripsit* and *scripseram* below. So in Münzer's
opinion Cicero had some previous information about the end of the
Epitome (perhaps from Hortensius[3]), which, as he shows,[4] might
well have given some details about the historian's career.

When Atticus proved that the consul and tribune was the son of a
Marcus, Cicero, says Münzer, deduced that the parental praenomina
given in the *Brutus* ought to be interchanged. But as the text of the
letter stands, the point which Atticus had disproved was the identity
of Laelius' relative with the historian. So Fraccaro insists, and so
Münzer himself explicitly admits.[5] How did Atticus' information
disprove that? Why did not Cicero, interchanging the praenomina,
continues none the less to identify Laelius' son-in-law with the
historian, as Gai filius? I cannot find a direct answer in Münzer's
paper, and can salve his logic only by crediting him with an un-
expressed assumption that Cicero and Atticus both knew from other
evidence that the father of the character in the *De Amicitia* was Marcus and not Gaius. If Cicero was determined for some reason not
apparent to apply the remaining fact mentioned in the *Brutus*,
authorship of a history, to a Fannius who was not the consul of 122,
he must in the light of Atticus' information make the historian son
of Gaius. But *ex hypothesi* Laelius' relative was son of Marcus.

[1] Pp. 435 ff.
[2] Kurfess rightly observes that a pluperfect would be needed.
[3] See p. 435, n.   [4] Pp. 434 f.   [5] P. 438.

Therefore they were different persons. But this solution could not be maintained in face of the Epitome now in his hands, confirming as it did his earlier information as to the historian's praenomen.[1]

Something like this may possibly have occurred. Fraccaro's theory that the historian was not the son of Marcus is certainly less plausible. For Cicero clearly believed that the epitome at his elbow proved, against Atticus, the identity of the historian with Laelius' son-in-law: *te autem nunc [refellit] Brutus et Fannius*. It must, therefore, have presented him as Marci filius. Considered, however, as a defence of the MS. text Münzer's explanation will not serve. Kurfess' interpretation of *scripsi*, 'Ich schrieb dir, was in der Fannius-epitome am Schluß stand', fails to account for the word order,[2] and it is not easy to see why Cicero should have so written to Atticus after the 'refutation', as the tenses imply. However this may be, the elephantine repetition *in Bruti epitome Fannianorum* when *quo in libro* lay to hand, remains incredible.

An explicable text could be obtained by following Bosius in *conturbat enim me epitome Bruti Fanniana* (*an Bruti epitome Fannianorum? scripsi quod erat in extremo*) and marking a lacuna before *idque*: e.g. ⟨*Fanni ipsius patrem Marcum esse ex Bruto cognoveram*⟩ *idque ego secutus* et sqq., but nobody would believe in it. Perhaps it is more likely that *Fanniana* represents *Caeliana*, assimilated to *Fannianorum*. Three or four days previously Cicero (now at Tusculum) had asked Atticus to send him a copy of Caelius Antipater's Annals as epitomized by Brutus: *epitomen Bruti Caelianorum velim mihi mittas* (13. 8), and we should expect to hear of him here. If this could be proved it would establish the view that Caelius wrote a general history down to the death of C. Gracchus as well as his work on the Second Punic War,[3] but of course it cannot. The passage should be obelized.

12. 7. 1   *vel nimia* liberalitate uti mea quam sua libertate

vel nimia M^2bdmsO^2: vel imma M, vellim mea R, velim magna P

---

[1] Münzer seems to think that the Epitome stated the historian's relationship with Laelius. In that case Cicero could hardly have failed to draw the right conclusion straight away.

[2] His alternative rendering of *in*, 'with regard to', is better, but his Ciceronian parallels do not convince. *de* would be the normal word.

[3] *RE*, IV. 1, 186 f.

velim magis of the old editions accounts for the conjectures *vellem magis* (Boot) and *vellet magis* (Orelli), but does not commend them. I see little to attract in *me eum malle* (Müller), and prefer *vel nimia ⟨malim⟩*, *malī* having dropped out between *mia* and *li*. *vel imma* of M is practically the same as *vel nimia* (equal number of vertical strokes).

12. 7. 2   de Balbo...simul ac redierit. sin ille tardius, ego tamen *triduum*, et, quod praeterii, Dolabella etiam mecum.

triduo would suit the context better: 'I shall come to Rome in two days' time.' *Dolabella etiam mecum* more naturally means 'Dolabella will come with me' than 'Dolabella will be with me (in Rome)', and Atticus would want to know the date of Cicero's arrival rather than the length of his stay. The change, like Wesenberg's *biduo* for *biduum* in 13. 30. 1, is not absolutely necessary; on the other hand, MSS. are continually confusing final *o* with final *um* as, for example, in 2. 16. 1 *primo/primum*, 4. 3. 4 *campo/campum*, 7. 18. 3 *amico/amicum*, 10. 12a. 3 *theatro/theatrum*, 4. 3. 3 *vestibulum/vestibulo*, 7. 11. 3 *annum/anno*, 9. 18. 3 *Arpinum/Arpino*, 10. 4. 10 *profectum/profecto*, 10. 4. 11 *eum/eo*, 10. 9. 1 *Pompeium/Pompeio*, 10. 15. 2 *Marcellum/Marcello*.

12. 9   cetera noli putare amabiliora fieri posse v⟨i⟩lla, litore, prospectu maris, *tum his* rebus omnibus.

The various conjectures seem needless. *tum* is all right syntactically, and the sense is not inept, as Ernesti thought, if *his rebus omnibus* be taken as the ensemble, opposed to the particular items. Lehmann's *tumulis* is especially unfortunate, not only because 'at Astura there is no rising ground that could even be called *tumuli*' (TP), but because it rests on an untenable belief that this word in 14. 13. 1 *utrum magis tumulis prospectuque an ambulatione ἀλιτενεῖ delecter* means the rising ground behind Cumae. As most people think, it means the mountains of Arpinum; and TP have no right to say that Cicero would have called them *montes*. The Alban hills, higher than any close to Arpinum, are called *tumuli* (*Mil.* 85, *Div.* 1. 18, Liv. 7. 24. 8); cf. also *Catil.* 2. 24 *Catilinae tumulis silvestribus*, Florus, 2. 12. 5 *Perrhaebosque tumulos*.

12. 32. 2   Publilia ad me scripsit matrem suam, cum Publilio
loqueretur, ad me cum illo venturam et se una, si ego paterer...
rescripsi mi etiam gravius esse quam tum cum illi dixissem me
solum esse velle. qua re nolle me hoc tempore eam ad me
venire. putabam, si nihil rescripsissem, illam cum matre venturam: nunc non puto. apparebat enim illas litteras non esse
ipsius. illud autem, quod fore video, ipsum volo vitare, ne *illi*
ad me veniant. et una est vitatio ut ego ⟨*evolem*⟩. nollem, sed
necesse est.

mi *Orelli*: me Ω   esse Δ*O*²: esse adfectum *ORP*   illi *RP*: ill(a)e Δ, *de O*
non liquet   evolem *addidi*, avolem (*vel* alio) *Madvig*

Neither *cum Publilio ut loquerer* (ed. Romana) nor *ut cum Publilio
loquerer* (Schmidt; Moricca in text) is palaeographically convincing.
I suspect that Junius' *locutam* contains part of the truth, and that
Cicero wrote something like *matrem suam cum Publilio* ⟨*locutam,
mecum ut*⟩ *loqueretur ad me* et sqq.

Tyrrell was right to read *illi* in 1891, though mistaken in claiming
it for his own. His example has not been followed, except by TP in
their first edition of 1897; in the second edition of 1915 it has sunk
without trace. Cicero thinks that his reply will put Publilia off,
since he can tell that her letter was dictated by her mother; had it
been genuinely hers, she might not be so easily discouraged. But he
is still troubled at the prospect of a visit from her mother and
brother, which he can avoid only by flight. For *illae*, which makes
him flatly contradict himself within a dozen words, Boot proposed,
but did not read, *illa* (*veniat*). *illi* (Publilius and his mother)
involves no conjectural change and has two merits besides: it
exactly fits the context, and persons imperfectly acquainted with the
Latin rules of gender may have thought it ungrammatical.

avolem is usually written after *ego*. *avolare* occurs once elsewhere
in the Correspondence, *evolare* six times (seven, if I have rightly
conjectured it in 14. 7. 2¹).

12. 44. 3   Philotimus nec Carteiae Pompeium teneri...bellumque
narrat reliquum satis magnum. solet omnino esse *Fulviniaster*.

Editors have been known to put *Fulviniaster* in their texts. There
is no Fulvinius in *RE*. Rejecting *Fulviaster*, ψευδομάρτυς, *Fulmi-*

¹ *Proc. Cam. Phil. Soc.* 1956–7, p. 17.

naster, φιλοτίμων (or *fumi*) μαστήρ, φιλομαθής, I propose *Favoni-aster*. This freedman's pose as a zealous optimate had been ridiculed before: 9. 7. 6 *Philotimo, homini forti ac nimium optimati*, 10. 9. 1 *quam saepe pro Pompeio mentientis.* Here Cicero calls him a 'Favonius *manqué*' because Favonius since Cato's death stood as the type of a republican zealot. So he does, apparently, in 15. 29. 2 *Quintus filius...mirus civis, ut tu Favonium Asinium dicas*, where *Asinium* may possibly be sound after all: 'so that by his side you might call Favonius Tom Fool'. For a play on *Asinius–asinus* cf. Apul. *Met.* 11. 27.[1]

12. 45. 1 in Tusculano eo commodius ero quod et crebrius tuas litteras accipiam et te ipsum nonnumquam videbo; nam ceteroqui ἀνεκτότερα erant Asturae. *nec* haec quae me refricant hic me magis angunt; etsi tamen, ubicumque sum, illa sunt mecum.

Cicero must not be made to say 'in every other way Astura was more tolerable than Tusculum, *and* reminders of loss hurt me in Tusculum no more than in Astura'. *nunc* (Corradus) seems otiose, and the vulgate is not salved by putting *nam...Asturae* in a parenthesis; for the point of adding 'yet wherever I am they are with me' would be gone if the memories of Tusculum were not especially painful. For *nec* read *et*, removing the full stop.

12. 52. 3 de lingua Latina securi es animi. dices: '*qui talia conscribis?*' ἀπόγραφα sunt, minore labore fiunt; verba tantum adfero, quibus abundo.

es *M²bdmsO²*: est *MOR*   talia conscribis *Mᶜbdms*, alia que scribis *MO*, talia que scribis *RO²*

So modern editors. But the reading and interpretation of this celebrated passage are quite uncertain. TP think that Atticus was concerned lest 'philosophical works composed so rapidly and under such circumstances could not in point of style be up to Ciceronian standard, and...might produce imitation and thus in a measure impair the Latin tongue'. If so he cannot have been much re-

---

[1] *Favonium Maximum* might be considered, however; *x* and *s* are often confused.

assured to hear that they were mere translations, done with no great pains. The old view, that Atticus is told not to worry about the difficulty of finding Latin equivalents for Greek terms, is hardly better. It means dissociating *qui talia conscribis*, 'how do you compile such works?', from what precedes. And after all this was not the reading of the archetype. I have sometimes wondered whether *lingua Latina* is Varro's work on the subject which he had promised to dedicate to Cicero more than two years previously (cf. 13. 12. 3), or even a work contemplated by Cicero himself, about which Atticus had implied that progress might be quicker. In that case the question should perhaps run *quid a⟨d i⟩lla quae scribis?*, 'What is such a book compared with your *Philosophica?*' But it is a case for the obelus.

BOOK XIII

13. 13. 2   volo Dolabellae valde desideranti; non reperio quid, et simul αἰδέομαι Τρῶας, neque, si *aliud quid*, potero μέμψιν effugere.

> aliud quid *bdm*: aliud qui *MRPC*, aliquid quid *s*

The usual reading *si aliquid* (Manutius) makes *neque...effugere* add nothing significant to αἰδέομαι Τρῶας. *si aliud quid* is easier to print (with Moricca) than to explain, but cf. 13. 10. 2 *ad Dolabellam, ut scribis, ita puto faciendum,* κοινότερα *quaedam et* πολιτικώτερα. *faciendum certe aliquid est; valde enim desiderat.* I think Cicero's meaning might be represented thus: 'I can't find a topic [of the kind proposed], and at the same time I am afraid of what people will think; and, if I choose something else [i.e. something non-political], I shall still be blamed for giving him a dedication at all.'

13. 20. 4   δεδῆχθαι te nollem quod nihil erat.

⟨*eo*⟩ *nollem* Wesenberg; so Boot and TP. But cf. Plaut. *Poen.* 572 *hau vostrumst iracundos esse quod dixi ioco,* Varr. *R.R.* 1. 59. 2 *cur non quod natura datum utantur,* Ov. *Met.* 6. 612 f. *sed ferro, sed si quid habes, quod vincere ferrum | possit,* 12. 93 f. *est aliquid non esse satum Nereide, sed qui | Nereaque et natas et totum temperat aequor.*

13. 21. 3   The last words are dubious. Perhaps thus:

vides quanto hoc diligentius curem quam aut de rumore aut de Pollione, de Pansa etiam. ⟨sed⟩ si quid certius; credo enim palam factum esse. de Critonio, si quid est certi; ne de Metello et Balbino.

> sed *addidi*   est certi Boot: esset certe Ω

With *certius* and *certi* supply *scribes*: cf. 13. 49. 1 *de Tigellio, si quid novi*, 10. 8. 10 *tu, si quid de Hispaniis certius . . . scribes. ne=ne dicam*. Boot (ed. 1) suggests that *dicam* may have fallen out before the following *dic mihi*, and this is quite possible. But, as he says, 'non valde requiritur'. Balbinus may be L. Cornelius Balbus the younger, like Balbillus in 15. 13. 4.[1]

13. 22. 4   ego, ut constitui, adero, atque utinam tu quoque eodem die! sin quid (multa enim), utique postridie. etenim coheredes; a quis sine te opprimi *militia* est. alteris iam litteris nihil ad me de Attica.

malitia (edd. vett.) will hardly do. The old view that it refers to Cicero's fellow heirs, plotting to get at him before Atticus could lend support, is plainly implausible. Tyrrell's *sine tua opprimi malitia! est alteris* et sqq. is highly praised by Reid,[2] who, however, thought *est* should be deleted. That means three considerable changes, and, after all, the exclamatory infinitive does not convince, despite the parallel for *malitia* in 15. 26. 4. It would be better to explain *malitia* as *iniuria* (cf. Ter. *H.T.* 796 *ius summum saepe summast malitia*), but there is no real parallel. Other attempts are *male tuti est*; *mi Tite aestuo*; *molestum est*; *stultitia est*; *mortis instar est*. Most editors obelize.

iniuria est would, in fact, be very close to the MSS. *iniu* in minuscule is very much the same as *mili*, so the change is hardly more than that of a single letter. But I cannot find that Cicero so used *iniuria*. The phrase in his day was *iniurium est* (*Off.* 3. 89 *quia sit iniurium*, Liv. 43. 5. 5, and often in Comedy). This he may well have written here, final *ū* becoming *a* as in 8. 11. 1 *consilium/-a*, 10. 8. 5 *iratum/rata*.

---

[1] *Proc. Cam. Phil. Soc.* 1956–7, p. 18.
[2] *Hermath.* X (1899), p. 346.

13. 23. 3   quamquam ista retentione omnis ait uti Trebatius. quid
tu istos putas? nosti *domum*. quare confice εὐαγώγως.

Reid's *dominum*, accepted by TP, is not a happy suggestion.
Cicero usually tended to think better of Caesar himself than of his
adherents. Besides there is nothing amiss with *domum*, 'the whole
gang', 'omnem illam familiam' (Gronovius). So in *Phil.* 3. 35
nostis insolentiam Antoni, nostis amicos, nostis totam domum, 12. 17
neque solum in ipsum, sed in eius socios facinorum et ministros, et
praesentes et eos qui una sunt, in totam denique M. Antoni domum sum
semper invectus. Cf. *domus* of a philosophical school, as in *Acad.*
1. 13 et al.

13. 24. 1   quid est quod Hermogenes mihi Clodius Andromenem
sibi dixisse se Ciceronem vidisse Corcyrae? ego enim audita
tibi *putaram*.

Cicero cannot have thought before hearing this report that
Atticus had heard it. If the tense were epistolary he would have
written *putabam*. Read either this (cf. 1. 19. 4 *liberabam/liberaram*,
9. 10. 3 *cogitaram/cogitabam*) or, better, *putarem*, 'I should have
thought you would have heard of it [and informed me, if it had been
true]': cf. 13. 25. 1 *de Andromene, ut scribis, ita putaram. scisses*
enim mihique dixisses.

13. 40. 1   itane? nuntiat Brutus illum ad bonos viros? εὐαγγέλια.
sed ubi eos? nisi forte se suspendit. hic autem *ut fultum est.*
ubi igitur φιλοτέχνημα illud tuum, quod vidi in Parthenone,
Ahalam et Brutum? sed quid faciat?

est om. RP

illum=Caesarem.

If *ut fultum est* is wrong it has yet to be emended: for nine failures,
see Moricca's apparatus. Perhaps it is right, after all. A partially
quoted proverb is often bound to be unintelligible unless the rest of
it is known, and a page or two of Petronius' banquet talk can show
how many ancient proverbs we have lost. *fabam mimum* (1. 16. 13),
cum suo tibicine (6. 1. 23), ὅτε ναῦς ἄνθρακες (15. 5. 1) are cases
where conservatism is really caution. If challenged to produce a
possible complement to *ut fultum est* which would suit the context,

I should suggest *sedet*: cf. Plaut. *Stich*. 94 *mane, pulvinum—bene procuras. mihi sati' sic fultum est*. 'As the cushions lie, so he sits' might be said of a man who in a particular situation takes the line conducive to his own comfort. Brutus thinks so well of Caesar (in August 45) because he knows which side his bread is buttered. So much for Atticus' φιλοτέχνημα (whatever that was). But after all what is he to do?

13. 41. 1   quod autem relanguisse *se* dicit, ego ei tuis litteris lectis
σκολιαῖς ἀπάταις significavi me non fore ⟨ἄτεγκτον⟩.
ἄτεγκτον *suppl. TP, alii alia*

Quintus junior had for some time been out of favour with his family. But Quintus senior had now been mollified (13. 39. 1), and was even proposing to give up his town house to his son, between whom and his mother Pomponia there was war.[1] Cicero had not been mollified, but had decided to pretend to be, σκολιαῖς ἀπάταις (13. 38. 2). Quintus senior is the subject of *dicit*.

quod can hardly mean 'because'. Atticus already knew of Quintus' relenting and had advised Cicero how to act in consequence. Cicero would not now give this same reason for taking the advice. To understand with Boot 'quod autem attinet ad id quod relanguisse se dicit' is no easier. Cicero's information about his own attitude is not apropos of what Quintus 'is saying' about his (Q.'s) sentiments towards Quintus junior. But it could be apropos of something said by Quintus, and reported by Atticus, about Cicero. In that case *me* should replace *se*, which will have come from *relanguisse*.

13. 46. 2   Balbum conveni...ex eo hoc primum: 'paulo ante
acceperam *eas* litteras, in quibus magnopere confirmat ante
ludos Romanos.' legi epistulam.

Balbus could hardly have said *eas*. He could have said *Caesaris* (Schütz before Boot). He probably said *has*.

---

[1] §1 *cum ille quereretur filio cum matre bellum et se ob eam causam domo cessurum filio diceret*, on which TP: 'It ought to mean that he would give up his house to his son. But what good would that be if son and mother were on bad terms with one another?' Answer with Corradus: '*cessurum*] cum uxore'. No need therefore for ⟨*de*⟩ *domo*.

13. 48. 1   heri nescio quid in strepitu videor *exaudisse, cum* diceres
te in Tusculanum venturum. quod utinam!

Reid's reason for proposing *quasi,*[1] that *cum* would only be
applicable if there were no doubt as to what was said, is nugatory. As
well read *quasi* in *N.D.* 1. 58 *saepe enim de Lucio Crasso illo familiari
tuo videor audisse, cum te togatis omnibus sine dubio anteferret* (for
videor cf. also *Fam.* 9. 8. 1 *quas a te probari intellexisse mihi videbar,*
Liv. 1. 23. 7 *audisse videor,* 40. 55. 3 *intellexisse videor*). The really
unusual feature is the absence of a personal pronoun (*te, ex te, a te,
de te*). Nowhere else is it lacking in the numerous examples of this
Ciceronian idiom, for which see Kühner–Stegmann II, p. 333.
I would not risk much on this passage as a genuine exception when
⟨*ex te*⟩ *exaudisse* lies to hand.[2]

BOOK XIV

14. 5. 1   illa signa non bona, si cum signis legiones veniunt ⟨e⟩
Gallia. quid tu illas putas, quae fuerunt in Hispania? nonne
idem postulaturas? quid, quas Annius *transportavit?* Caninium
volui, sed μνημονικὸν ἁμάρτημα.

transportavit *b*²: -tavi *MdsRP,* -tam *bm*   ea nimium *P*

Without doubt Boot's *C. Asinium volui* is substantially right;
Cicero corrects his own slip. For *volui* cf. *Cael.* 32 *cum istius mulieris
viro—fratrem volui dicere; semper hic erro,* Plaut. *Cas.* 367 *dum 'mihi'
volui 'huic' dixi,* 702 *ut nubat mihi—illud quidem volebam, nostro
vilico.* A letter of Byron's is dated 'August—September I mean—1'.[3]
Perhaps Cicero momentarily confused two Pollios, since this cognomen appears in the *gens Annia* in the Augustan period and after.
But the praenomen should be discarded. Cicero in his letters calls
Asinius Pollio by his nomen or his cognomen or both together, but
never C. Asinius. No doubt Boot and the editors who follow him
thought they were obeying the *ductus litterarum,* but in fact they

---

[1] *Hermath.* x (1899), p. 355.
[2] Or *ex* ⟨*te*⟩ *audisse.* But the compound verb, 'catch', suits this context.
[3] Prothero, vol. II, p. 256.

were doing nothing of the kind. The initial *c* of *Caninium* in the MSS. represents the missing final *t* of *transportavit*. Read then *Asinium volui*.

14. 10. 3 quod quaeris iamne ad centena Cluvianum, adventare videtur. *sed* primo anno LXXX detersimus.

Editors are satisfied with Wesenberg's false premise: 'ego, quoniam non contrarii quidquam adiungitur, sed causa, cur ad C adventare videri dicatur, pro *sed* scribo *sc*.'[1] Cicero means: 'it looks as if it is approaching that, but in the first year we have cleared [not 100,000 but] 80,000'.

14. 12. 1 verum illuc *refero*. tam claram tamque testatam rem tamque iustam, Buthrotiam, non tenebimus aliqua ex parte? et eo quidem magis quo *ista* plura?

Up to this point Cicero has been complaining of arbitrary grants by Antony, made under the pretext of carrying out Caesar's alleged decisions. Now he turns to Atticus' 'Buthrotian business', which lay in getting implemented a written promise by Caesar to remit a sentence of confiscation against the Buthrotians. Modern editors[2] who keep *refero* in preference to *referor, redeo, revertor, ⟨me⟩ refero*, follow Lehmann in understanding *me* after the analogy of *recipere= se recipere* in old Latin. I would sooner understand 'but I apply all this to the following purpose'. If the Sicilians and Deiotarus benefited from Caesar's supposititious benevolence, this at any rate strengthened the case for the fulfilment of Caesar's undeniable pledge to Atticus. So substantially Corradus and Manutius, and more latterly Boot, but he changed his mind in his second edition. I must admit that *referre* in this sense is generally used of the subject's own actions or desires, but the extension seems natural.

iste (Victorius, edd.) may be right, but there is nothing obviously amiss with *ista*: 'the more of such goings on there are'.

14. 13. 5 scribis enim esse rumores me ad lacum quod habeo venditurum, minusculam vero villam *utique* Quinto traditurum vel impenso pretio.

utique *om. bdmsE, del. Mᶜ*

[1] *Emend.* p. 98.   [2] TP, Winstedt, Moricca.

Most editors have omitted *utique*, thinking it, with Graevius, no loss. That is because they have not caught the point. The rumours were that Cicero would sell to Quintus his villa on the Lucrine Lake, but that, if he did not do this, he would at any rate (*utique*) hand over to him the 'cottage' (probably on the Puteolanum).

14. 16. 1   ipse autem eo die in Paeti nostri tyrotarichum immine-
bam; *perpaucis diebus in Pompeianum*, post in haec Puteolana
et Cumana regna renavigaro.

The editors who keep *perpaucis diebus in Pompeianum* do not tell us what it means. Not, apparently, 'in a very few days I shall go to Pompeii', for Cicero arrived there next day (14. 17. 1). Müller, who obelizes, thought *perpaucos dies in Pompeiano* of Wesenberg and Boot remarkably audacious. *Pompeiano* is not audacious (see on 12. 7. 2), and *perpaucos dies* is perhaps unnecessary. The ablative for duration of time has been denied to Cicero, but ingenuity has to be strained to do it: see Kühner–Stegmann I, pp. 360 ff. So perhaps read *perpaucis diebus in Pompeiano* [sc. *ero*]; cf. Plin. *Ep.* 4. 13. 1 *ipse pauculis adhuc diebus in Tusculano commorabor.*

14. 16. 2   sed ad rem ut veniam, o Dolabellae nostri magnam
ἀριστείαν! quanta est ἀναθεώρησις! ...mihi quidem videtur
Brutus noster iam vel coronam auream per forum ferre posse.
quis enim audeat violare proposita cruce aut saxo, praesertim
tantis plausibus, tanta approbatione *infimorum?*

infimorum *bs*: infirmorum *cett.*

Castiglioni's ⟨*etiam*⟩ *infimorum* raises a point which arises also in 4. 1. 5 *gradus templorum ab infima* (*infimo* Lehmann) *plebe completi erant.* If *infimus* in such contexts had a markedly pejorative force the proposed changes would be needed, but other passages suggest that *infimi* or *infima plebs* means little worse than *vulgus*, 'the lower orders': Liv. 33. 46. 6 *ut secundis auribus accipi orationem animad-vertit, et infimorum quoque libertati gravem esse superbiam eorum*, Ascon. 40 *quo facto et plebem infimam offenderat et senatus magnam gratiam inierat* (cf. ibid. 28 *infimaeque plebis*, Curt. 10. 7. 1, Tac. *Hist.* 2. 38 *e plebe infima C. Marius*, Suet. *Otho*, 7. 1 *ab infima plebe appellatus Nero*, Cic. *Mil.* 95 *infimam multitudinem*), where *plebs infima* balances *senatus* as *infimus quisque* balances *boni omnes* in 14. 17 A. 7.

The MSS. and recent texts offer the same common corruption, *infirmi* for *infimi*, in 4. 2. 3.

14. 19. 1 (8 May 44) sed cum Dolabellae *aritia* (sic enim tu ad me scripseras) magna desperatione adfectus essem, ecce tibi et Bruti et tuae litterae! ille exilium meditari. nos autem alium portum propiorem huic aetati videbamus; in quem mallem equidem pervehi florente Bruto nostro constitutaque re p., sed nunc quidem, ut scribis, non utrumvis. adsentiris enim mihi nostram aetatem a castris, praesertim civilibus, abhorrere.

On *aritia* Moricca points to TP: 'cf. quae acute isti docti viri disseruerunt ad l.' I would say 'guarda e passa', were it not that *aritia* stands unobelized in the best of modern texts, C. F. W. Müller's. The kernel of TP's note is this:

The fact is that *aritia* is probably the very word which Cicero wrote. Atticus had through inadvertence written *aritia* for *avaritia*. Cicero now deliberately makes the same mistake, explaining to Atticus why he does so. It must be remembered that *avaritia* would be pronounced *auritia*, as we may infer from the story about the fig-seller who was crying figs, *cauneas*, just as Crassus was starting on his fatal expedition to Parthia, and who was understood by the people in the street to be crying *cave ne eas*.[1]

A central misunderstanding here is responsible not only for the retention of *aritia* but also for a quantity of bad conjectures— *avaritia*, ἀτισία, ἀπορία, ἀπιστία, ἀργία, *artitia*, ἀσιτία, ἀκρισία, ἀρρησία, *malitia*. Even the right word, ἀριστεία, was supposed by Friedrich Schmidt, to whom it is usually credited,[2] to make ironical reference to Dolabella's failure to pay his debt to Cicero, and by his namesake Otto Eduard to mean 'solvency'. This paragraph is not concerned with debts but with politics, and to Cicero the great political event of the previous fortnight had been Dolabella's drastic

---

[1] And not *cavā ne eas*. But that was in Brundisium, not Dublin.
[2] Victorius had thought of it in its true sense. See below.

action against the Caesarian mob in Rome. As TP[1] record, 'Cicero was in the wildest delight at this (as he considered) heroic deed... and on May 3 wrote an over-enthusiastic letter[2] to that violent self-seeker'. Cf. 14. 15. 1 (1 May) *o mirificum Dolabellam meum!...* *magnam ἀναθεώρησιν res habet...quid quaeris? heroica,* 14. 16. 2 (2 May) *o Dolabellae nostri magnam ἀριστείαν!, Fam.* 12. 1. 1 (3 May, to Cassius) *re publica a Dolabella meo praeclarissime gesta.* Obviously he is saying here that after all this elation Atticus' and Brutus' letters arrived like a cold douche. For Dolabella's conduct it is as certain as anything in these matters can be that he uses, in its proper sense, the same term ἀριστεία as in 14. 16. 2.[3]

Why does he add *sic enim tu ad me scripseras?* No doubt ἀριστεία was originally (note the pluperfect) Atticus' expression, but Cicero has a reason for reminding him of it. Atticus had thought his eulogies of Dolabella too enthusiastic, as they were, and *sic...scripseras* is a reminder that ἀριστεία was after all the term Atticus had used.[4] So in §5 *venio ad recentiores litteras...'me facere magnam* πρᾶξιν *Dolabellae'. mihi mehercule ita videtur; non potuit esse maior tali re talique tempore. sed tamen, quicquid ei tribuo, tribuo ex tuis litteris. tibi vero adsentior maiorem* πρᾶξιν[5] *eius fore, si mihi quod debuit[6] dissolverit.* The joking reference to Dolabella's debt is taken up next day, 14. 18. 1: *saepius me iam agitas quod rem gestam Dolabellae nimis in caelum videar efferre. ego autem, quamquam sane probo factum, tamen, ut tantopere laudarem, adductus sum tuis et unis et alteris litteris. sed totum se a te abalienavit Dolabella ea de causa qua me quoque sibi inimicissimum reddidit. o hominem pudentem! Kal. Ian. debuit: adhuc non solvit, praesertim cum se maximo aere alieno Faberii manu liberarit et opem ab Ope petierit. licet enim iocari ne me valde conturbatum putes.* But 14. 19. 1 is not a jocular paragraph.

Now there is Victorius' point to meet: 'ne *Aristia* legas, repugnat

---

[1] Vol. v, p. lxviii.

[2] 14. 17A=*Fam.* 9. 4.

[3] With the ἀριστεῖαι of the Iliad in mind (see Liddell–Scott–Jones s.v.). Do commentators think this too elementary to mention?

[4] Cicero uses it again in 16. 9 *metuo ne quae* ἀριστεία *me absente.*

[5] I think πρᾶξιν probably *has* a double sense, though, as TP note, 'the joke does not proceed quite completely'.

[6] Malaespina's *debet* is not needed. *debuit=debere coepit:* cf. 14. 18. 1 *Kal. Ian. debuit: adhuc non solvit.*

ut arbitror illud, quod se magna ob eam rem desperatione affectum esse dicit'. True enough. But *desperatione affectus* contradicts, not only ἀριστείᾳ, but the whole drift of the paragraph. *ecce tibi* demands a reversal; the gloom induced by the letters must, if only on stylistic grounds, have followed not despair but hope. A fleeting visitation of common sense led TP to think of altering *adfectus* to *refectus*, 'though that would be a violent proceeding'. As a matter of fact, apparently dissimilar prefixes are not rarely confused. To speak only of *ad-* and *re-*, all the MSS. have *repetitor* for *competitor* in 4. 17. 2 (on *restitisse/constitisse* in 2. 24. 2 see ad loc.), and some have *oppressisset* for *repressisset* in 10. 9. 1. *per* replaces *re* in 10. 16. 1 (*remisissem*), and *re* replaces *per* in 2. 16. 4 (*perscripseram*). *expiscere* becomes *respicere* in 2. 17. 3. In 11. 8. 2 the Würzburg fragments confirm Corradus' *conficiar* against *afficiar* of the other MSS.; *affirmatior* has replaced *obfirmatior* in 1. 11. 1, *attulerit* (in bds) *obtulerit* in 2. 22. 1. For *re* confused with *de* (whence *ad*) Professor Watt refers me to Müller's note on *Sest.* p. 64. 8. *refectus*, then, may be the answer, but in that case *e* is required before *magna.*[1] *ex* need not then be added, with Cratander and many editors, before *Dolabellae.*

There are no textual problems in the rest of the passage, but fogs of misinterpretation persist. The 'other haven' is death (so Manutius and others): cf. *Sen.* 71 *ut quo propius ad mortem accedam, quasi terram videre videar aliquandoque in portum ex longa navigatione esse venturus, Tusc.* 1. 118 *portum potius paratum nobis et perfugium putamus* (sim. Sen. *Dial.* 7. 19. 1, *Ep.* 70. 3, Plin. *N.H.* 25. 24 *ea condicio vitae est ut mori plerumque etiam optimis portus sit*). He would rather put it off until Brutus had restored the republic. But this time no choice is offered, i.e. he cannot choose, as in 49 he could, between neutrality and fighting with the republicans. If he is to stay alive, he *must* join Brutus. Death is therefore his only refuge, for he cannot fight at his time of life.

utrumvis was understood in the sixteenth century: 'non licet nunc mihi, quod Caesaris bello licuit, non interesse civili bello' (Manutius). And the twentieth? 'He may refer to death...but, as Dr. Reid points out, his statement that he has a choice, and the words *nostram*

---

[1] *magna de re p. spei elatione* had occurred to me (*r* and *l* are quite often confused). But *spei elatio* (cf. *animi elatio*) lacks confirmation.

aetatem following *huic aetati*, render that supposition unlikely.' The trouble is that when Cicero writes *utrumvis (licet)* he is apt to leave the formulation of the alternatives to the intelligence of his readers. As here, so in *Verr.* 2. 3. 167 *nihil dicet ex tempore, nihil ex sua voluntate, nihil cum utrumvis licuisse videatur* his presumption is punished. Editors[1] interrupt him with an, at best, misleading comma before *cum*, and L. H. G. Greenwood makes him babble.[2] Only analogy and the context show that *nihil...videatur* means 'he will say nothing in circumstances where he might seem to have the option of speech or silence' (it is a *letter* to Verres that constitutes the man's evidence). Other examples of this idiom, though essentially similar, are harder to misunderstand: 9. 1. 4 *ego unus cui utrumvis liceret* (to leave Italy or stay), *Rosc. Am.* 4 *quod a ceteris forsitan ita petitum sit ut dicerent ut utrumvis* ('speak or not speak') *salvo officio se facere posse arbitrarentur*, ibid. 83 *si mihi liberet accusare, accusarem alios...quod certum est non facere, dum utrumvis licebit, Cael.* 2 *nec descensurum quemquam ad hanc accusationem fuisse cui utrum vellet liceret, Vat.* 34 *teque, cum tibi utrum velles liceret, dictitaris causam dicere maluisse*, Plaut. *Bacch.* 342 *censebam me ecfugisse a vita marituma, | ne navigarem tandem hoc aetatis senex; | id mi haud utrum velim licere intellego*, Quint. *Inst.* 5. 13. 6 *apud principem aliumve cui utrum velit liceat* ('who may acquit or condemn as he likes').

But here there ought to be no need for Manutius or for me. Cicero interprets himself six days later: 14. 22. 2 *neque enim iam*[3] *quod tibi tum licuit nobis nunc licebit. nam aperte laetati sumus. deinde habent in ore nos ingratos. nullo modo licebit quod tum et tibi licuit et multis.* φαινοπροσωπητέον *ergo et* ἰτέον *in castra? miliens mori melius, huic praesertim aetati.*

14. 20. 3   quod errare me putas, qui rem p. putem pendere ⟨e⟩
Bruto, sic se res habet: aut nulla erit aut ab isto istisve servabitur.

istiusve Ω (-ne *E*), *corr. edd. vett.*

[1] A. Klotz is an exception.
[2] De Mirmont's mistranslation is not foolish.
[3] So Victorius for *ne gemam*. But *iam...nunc* is awkward. Perhaps simply *neque* (or rather, as Professor Watt suggests, *nec*) *enim*.

istiusve is in the latest text, Moricca's. It is construable, 'by him
or his friends',[1] but we should expect *istiusque*—Brutus cannot be
excluded. §4 *quidnam istis agendum putem*, 14. 22. 2 *dicuntur...
milites...comparati*[2] *et quidem in istos* speak for *istis*, i.e. the con-
spirators, primarily Brutus and Cassius. For the intrusive *u* cf.
9. 10. 4 *d*[*u*]*as*, 11. 16. 1 *f*[*u*]*it*, 12. 46. 2 *pot*[*u*]*erunt*.

BOOK XV

15. 1. 4   istam vero, quam tibi molestam scribis esse, auditam a te esse
omnino demiror. nam quod eam conlaudavi apud amicos...
τί ἐκ τούτου; [quid est hoc] *quid est autem cur ego personatus
ambulem?* parumne foeda persona est ipsius senectutis?

ΤΟΕΣΤΟΥΟΥ *MRP*, τὸ ἐκ τούτου *Z*[1]: corr. *Kayser*

Following Palmer, modern editors take *quid est autem...
ambulem* for a dramatic verse, but neither they nor their predecessors
have provided a plausible interpretation. I believe these words are
Cicero's. Some woman with an ambition to succeed Publilia had
pestered Atticus, who remarked in his letter that Cicero had better
go about masked in future since women found him irresistible.
Cicero rejoins, 'Surely an old man like me doesn't need a mask to
make him ugly'. I wonder how many more *senarii* will come to
light. Casting at random I chance on two in 13. 21 a, § 1 *placetne tibi
primum edere iniussu meo* and §4 *accedit enim quod patrem, ut scire te
puto*.

15. 2. 4   Flamma quod bene loquitur, non moleste fero. Tyndari-
tanorum causa, de qua *causa* laborat, quae sit ignoro. hos
tamen...

de qua tam laborat *bms*

Lehmann's[3] Ciceronian examples of antecedent repeated in
relative clause suffice for editors. But one relative clause is not

---

[1] So Winstedt (reading *istisve*) 'or he and his party will save it'. Hardly
'soldiers'. Brutus had no soldiers in May 44.
[2] *comparari* Corradus. But here I agree with Moricca (and Boot, ed. 1) that
no change is needed.
[3] *Quaest. Tull.* pp. 113 f. See also Kühner–Stegmann II, pp. 283 f.

necessarily as good as another, and I think Cicero only used this
trick in those which can bear an added touch of interest or solemnity,
hence very rarely in a familiar letter.[1] Nothing could less deserve
emphasis than *de qua laborat*. Besides would not Cicero have
written *qua de causa?*

causa should be deleted as a common type of rewriting: see
Müller, pp. x–xii. Less likely, it conceals a name, *Casca* (Boot) or
Pansa (cod. Ursini).

The aposiopesis could hardly have meant anything even to Atticus. Possibly *vos tamen*, 'you people in Rome will settle it'. For the
ellipse cf. 13. 22. 4 *verum hoc quoque ut censueris, quippe qui omnia*.

15. 4. 2   redeamus igitur, *quoniam* saepe usurpas, ad Tusculanas
disputationes.

usurpas needs an object. *quoniam* ($q\overline{m}$) should give way to *quod*
($q\overline{d}$) as in *Fam.* 1. 1. 1. For this confusion Professor Watt refers me
to Sjögren, *Eranos*, XIX (1919–20), p. 144.

15. 5. 1   Cassius vero vehementer *orat ac petit* ut Hirtium quam
optimum faciam. sanum putas? ὅτε ναῦς ἄνθρακες.

It would indeed 'be rash to correct *orat* to *errat* with Lambinus'
(TP).[2] Better an inversion *petit atque orat* (see Orelli): cf. Pl. *Asin.*
662, 686 *petere atque orare*, Caes. *B.C.* 1. 17. 1 *petant atque orent*, *Bell.*
Afr. 77. 1 *petunt orantque*, Petr. 17. 9 *petoque et oro*, *Fam.* 9. 13. 3
peto igitur a te vel, si pateris, oro. But Orelli seems to be right when
he says 'haec non constanter observantur', though his only
example, Caes. *B.C.* 1. 32. 7 *orat ac postulat*, is a misreading; Caesar
wrote *hortatur*. Put in place of that *Bell. Afr.* 33. 1 *tantum orare et*
petere, Pl. *Rud.* 629 *teque oro et quaeso*. Perhaps the anticlimax is only
apparent and *(te) oro et peto* strictly meant 'I pray (to you), and ask
as my petition that. . .': cf. Front. *Strat.* 1. 11. 11 *signum modicae*
magnitudinis, quod Delphis sustulerat, orabat petebatque promissam
victoriam maturaret.

As for ὅτε ναῦς ἄνθρακες, I should leave it alone as Moricca does.
It is dangerous to tamper with a half-quoted proverb.

---

[1] Two of Lehmann's examples, *Att.* 15. 1a. 1 and *Fam.* 13. 58 come under
that head.
[2] Lambinus read *errat: petit*.

15. 6. 1 cum ad me Brutus noster scripsisset et Cassius, ut Hirtium, qui adhuc bonus *fuisset* (*sciebam* neque eum confidebam fore mea auctoritate meliorem; Antonio est enim fortasse iratior, causae vero amicissimus), tamen ad eum scripsi, *et sqq.*

qui adhuc bonus fuisset sciebam...confidebam *M*: quem adhuc bonum fuisse sciebant...confidebant *cett.* (bonum civem *s*)

This punctuation of Reid's is followed by TP and Moricca. It is certainly wrong, not because of the anacoluthon, but because *sciebam* belies Cicero's opinion of Hirtius' politics which at this time was uniformly unfavourable: 14. 20. 4 *quod Hirtium per me meliorem fieri volunt, do equidem operam, et ille optime loquitur, sed vivit habitatque cum Balbo, qui item bene loquitur. quid credas videris,* 14. 21. 4 *sic hominem traducere ad optimates paro.* λῆρος πολύς. *nemo est istorum qui otium non timeat,* 15. 1. 3 οὐδὲν ὑγιές, 15 5. 1 (see above). Madvig brings the right sense *qui adhuc bonus fuisset* ⟨*confirmarem et excitarem, etsi alieno a causa animo fuisse*⟩ *sciebam,* but it can be done more neatly: *qui adhuc bonus fuisset* ⟨*meliorem facerem, quem neque adhuc bonum fuisse*⟩ *sciebam, et sqq.*

15. 6. 3 (Hirtius) retine, obsecro te, Cicero, illos et noli sinere haec omnia perire, quae funditus ⟨medius⟩ fidius rapinis, incendiis, caedibus *pervertuntur.* tantum, si quid timent, caveant, nihil praeterea moliantur.

quae...pervertuntur, if a statement of fact, is a monstrous exaggeration of anything that was going on in Italy in May 44. Nor is it easy to understand an expression of intention merely, as Billerbeck does: 'Was man ohnehin schon bemüht ist...von Grund aus umzukehren.' These were calamities which would occur if Brutus and Cassius (*illos*) left to organize civil war. Perhaps *pervertentur.*

15. 8. 2 sed aliquid crastinus dies ad cogitandum nobis *dare*

dabit *P*

To read *dabit* seems unscientific, and there is little to be said for *dederit* or *adferet.* Bosius' *de ea re* is a limp superfluity. *debet* for *sed,* an old reading now credited to Madvig, is better, as Boot says (*de,* as Madvig says, might have been lost in the preceding *videndae*): not so *solet* (Ziehen). The simplest remedy is *sed* (*set*) ⟨*debet*⟩.

15. 9. 1   ait autem eodem tempore decretum iri ut et his et reliquis praetoriis provinciae decernantur. hoc certe melius quam illa Περσικὴ porticus; *nolo enim Lacedaemonem longinquo quo in Lanuvium existimavit.* 'rides', inquies, 'in talibus rebus?' quid faciam? plorando fessus sum.

nolo] nullo *R*   quo in *MsR*: quom *M^c msZ^b*, cum *b*, quin *d*   longinquo exulare quam in lavinum existimant *P*

Conjectures cluster like flies round this corrupt jest about Brutus' property at Lanuvium, with its Eurotas and its στοὰ Περσική. TP prefer, though they do not print, Gronovius', which is perhaps the silliest: *nolo enim Lacedaemonem longinquiorem Lanuvio existimaris*, 'you must understand that when I speak of Lacedaemon, I mean one no further off than Lanuvium'—as though Atticus needed such an explanation, or would have thought it amusing. Cicero *could* at least have written *nullam enim Lacedaemonem longinquiorem quam Lanuvinam existimaris*, 'don't imagine that any Sparta (even the real one) is further away than the one at Lanuvium', i.e., Brutus in his retreat (which he very possibly called 'Lacedaemon') is so cut off that he might as well be overseas.

15. 13. 4   de Bruto te nihil scire dicis, sed Servilia venisse M. Scaptium eumque *non qua pompa*, ad se tamen clam venturum sciturumque me omnia.

Servilia] selicia vel sim. Ω., corr. Corradus

Reid's *non* ⟨*anti*⟩*qua pompa* seems to me the best of the numerous conjectures, certainly better than *adsuevisset* (Lehmann) or *soleret* (Wesenberg) added after *pompa*. As a palaeographical improvement I suggest *non qua* ⟨*quondam*⟩ *pompa*, for *qdā* would easily disappear after *qua*.

15. 13a. 1   sed ait totum negotium Sestium nostrum suscepisse, optimum quidem illum virum nostrique amantissimum.

'Madvigius ad Fin. p. 545 recte pronomen particulae in hac forma subiici negat.' So Boot, who reads *illum quidem*, like R. Klotz (ed.

1), Baiter, and Wesenberg. What Madvig actually says is that Beier on *Orat.* 13 *multis quidem illa adiumentis* had legitimate doubts. He himself cites *Att.* 15. 13a. 1 and *Fam.* 16. 21. 6. Four more Ciceronian examples are cited by J. Samuelsson,[1] who is mistaken in thinking that Livy has only one (2. 24. 4). Add 28. 42. 5 *dux tumultuarius quidem ille L. Marcius* and 42. 8. 1 *nihil quidem illi pacti*; also Florus, 2. 6. 36 *magnis quidem illi proeliis,* Apul. *Met.* 6. 12. 1 *non obsequium quidem illa functura.*

15. 14. 2 (To Dolabella) postea vero quam ipse Atticus ad me venit in Tusculanum huius unius rei causa, tibi ut apud me gratias ageret, cuius eximiam quandam et admirabilem in causa Buthrotia voluntatem et singularem erga *me* amorem perspexisset, teneri non potui quin tibi apertius illud idem his litteris declararem. ex omnibus enim, mi Dolabella, studiis in me et officiis, quae summa sunt, hoc scito mihi et amplissimum videri et gratissimum esse, quod perfeceris ut Atticus intellegeret quantum ego *te,* quantum tu me amares.

me amorem $M^c bdms Z^t$: ea morem M, se amorem $M^2 ERP$

erga se sits snugly in our texts, padded by the habit of four centuries; down in the apparatus *erga me* waits for a voice to plead that Dolabella's zeal in the Buthrotian affair was at Cicero's behest, that he never seems to have been on close terms with Atticus, and that if he had been on such terms Cicero's mediation would not have been required and Atticus' thanks would have been expressed direct.

In the second sentence MSS. unite in error with editors, and only reason and analogy prove *te* wrong and *se* right. Cicero had bestirred himself for Atticus' sake and Dolabella for Cicero's, but not Cicero for Dolabella's. Nor could Cicero's love for Dolabella be proved to Atticus through favours conferred by Dolabella upon Atticus at Cicero's instigation. That for reason, this for analogy: *Fam.* 13. 47 *si ita tractaris Egnatium ut sentiat et se a me et me a te amari,* 13. 75 *ut Avianius, quoniam se a me amari putat, me a te amari sciat,* Plin. *Ep.* 1. 24. 5 *quo magis scires quantum esset illi mihi, ego tibi debiturus,* 6. 8. 9 *oro des operam ne ille se . . . a me, ego me neglectum a te putem.*

For confusion of pronouns cf. *se* for *me* in 10. 15. 3, *a me tibi* for *a te mihi* in 7. 7. 1, *tibi* for *sibi* in 11. 6. 1. See also on 13. 41. 1.

[1] *Eranos,* 1908, pp. 56 f. Cf. Leumann–Hofmann, p. 665.

15. 15. 1 nummos Arpinatium, si L. Fadius aedilis petet, vel omnis
reddito. ego ad te alia epistula scripsi ⟨de⟩ HS c̅x̅, quae Statio
curarentur. si ergo petet Fadius, ei volo reddi: praeter Fadium,
nemini. apud *me item* puto depositum. id scripsi ad Erotem ut
redderet.

me item is corrupt, as almost everyone admits. Conjectures
generally have followed in the wake of Lambinus: 'post vocem
depositum videntur deesse notae, quae significabant, quantum esset
depositum', or Bosius: 'in voc. *item* latere numeralem notam'.
I wonder whether *me item* comes from *Monetam*. Since the Mint
was a temple, private monies may have been deposited there. Possibly this bears on 8. 7. 3 *ad Philotimum scripsi de viatico, sive a
Moneta—nemo enim solvit—sive ab Oppiis*, though commentators
there have another explanation.

15. 18. 2 intellego te distentissimum esse qua de Buthrotis qua de
Bruto, cuius etiam ludorum *suorum* curam *etiam* administra-
tionem suspicor ex magna parte ad te pertinere.

etiam *Δ*, et *P*

To delete *suorum*, as Manutius wished to do and Lambinus did
before Baiter, is simple but unsatisfying. There is nothing to be said
for *scenicorum* in Lambinus' margin or *seorsum* (Bosius). Müller and
others adopt Lehmann's *sumptuosorum*, but it is not a Latin habit
thus to use adjectives for irrelevant comment. *istorum* might be
better; but after all it is possible to construe *cuius curam ludorum
suorum*, 'whose trouble over his games'.

et iam (in TP's first edition, also attributed to (R.) Klotz) may be
right: 'and indeed the management'. For *et iam* thus see Lewis–
Short s.v., II. C. 2. I am not sure that 5. 10. 3 should not read *etsi haec
ipsa fero equidem, et iam* [*etiam Ω*] *fronte, ut puto et volo, belle*.

15. 19. 2 hoc enimvero nunc discere aveo; *hoc* ego quid sit inter-
pretari non possum.

Do editors take the second *hoc* for a touch of rhetoric, or for
accidental surplusage? Either way, I find it hard to tolerate as Cicero's
and easy to omit as a copyist's repetition.

15. 20. 1   Dolabellae mandata sint quaelibet, *mihi* aliquid, vel quod
Niciae nuntiem. quis enim haec, ut scribis, *anteno?* nunc
dubitare quemquam prudentem quin meus discessus despera-
tionis sit, non legationis?

anteno *ΔZᵇ*, aut eno *R*, ante nos *P*

Manutius before Reid had *modo* (m̄) for *mihi* (m̄). It is practically
certain: cf. 13. 7 *rescribes igitur quicquid voles, dummodo quid,*
10. 15. 3 *quivis licet, dummodo aliquis.*

Half a dozen Greek conjectures have been proposed for *anteno.*
Add ἂν κινοῖ. Nobody would call in question Cicero's instructions
from Dolabella whatever they were, because everybody knew that
the proposed *legatio* was a matter of form. For κινεῖν thus see
Liddell–Scott–Jones s.v., II. 1.

15. 21. 2   ἐποχὴν vestram de re Cani *deliberationis* probo.

TP's explanation of *deliberationis* may not be to every editor's
taste: 'probably a gloss on ἐποχή [*sic*], the genitive being used, as
there might be a "suspension" of other things besides discussion'.
But a gloss editors are determined to have it. *deliberantium* (Moser)
and ⟨*quae est*⟩ *deliberationis* (Reid) are palaeographically less com-
mendable than a parenthetic *deliberationis* ⟨*enim*⟩;[1] for examples of
enim omitted cf. 7. 3. 10, 8. 11 D. 8, 11. 8. 1, 16. 4. 4 and for the
genitive 8. 12. 3 *etsi erat deliberationis,* 7. 10 *consilii res est* (sim. Caes.
B.G. 7. 38. 7, Liv. 22. 53. 6), *De Or.* 2. 330 *id est consilii.*

15. 22   quid ad haec Pansa? *utro* erit, si bellum erit?

vero *P*, cum utro *cod. Ursini*

utrobi (*utrubi*), *utrorum, utro ierit* (=*ibit*), *utro conferet se, intererit*
have been proposed. By analogy 'on which side' ought to be *utrā.*
This apparently occurs nowhere else, but that hardly signifies. *utro*
also is rare. Cicero has it once (*Parad.* 24); the other two examples
cited by dictionaries are supplied by Ovid and the elder Pliny.
utrubi is ante- and post-classical, *utrasque, utrinde, utrolibet* and
utrālibet all extremely rare. *utrāque,* on the other hand, comes (to

---

[1] Professor Watt thinks that *est* must be expressed and proposes ⟨*est enim*⟩
deliberationis or *deliberationis* ⟨*enim est*⟩. Cf. 15. 26. 5 fin.

say nothing of non-classical writing) three times in Lucretius and
once in Manilius (2. 904); also, where neither Housman nor dictionaries have noticed it, in Sil. 11. 477. It would be obscurantist to
deny that *utrā* must have existed and that Cicero would have used it
when he found occasion. Confusion of final *a* and *o* is too common
for illustration.

15. 23 (23 or 24 June 44)   Pansa si *tuae* rescripserit, et meam tibi et
illius epistulam mittam.

si tuere scripserit *Md*, sic (sit *m*) vere (vero *ms*) scripserit *msRP*

'Pansa, in replying to the letter of Atticus, would send his letter to
Cicero to be forwarded by the latter to Atticus' (TP). Why? 'ut
celerius vel tutius ad illum perveniret' (Boot). We do not know for
certain where Pansa was at this time, but a week previously he was in
Naples (15. 1. 3). If he was writing to Atticus it is unlikely on the
face of it that he would have found it quicker and safer to send his
letter to Cicero at Tusculum rather than direct to Rome. *meam* too
makes it overwhelmingly probable that the letter to which Cicero
looked for a reply was his own. Hence the conjectures *si*, *si mihi*,
sicubi, *si tum*, *si ante*. Better *si quae*; cf. *Fam.* 1. 4. 2 *si quae cona-
buntur agere*. *quo* is found for *tu* in 10. 8B. 2, *quis* for *civis* in 2. 12. 4.

15. 25. 1   uelim etiam scire quo die *Olympiacum* mysteria.

olympiacum (-tum *Δ*), olimpia cum *RP*

The simplest remedy here would be *quo die Olympia, tum
mysteria*, 'the date of the Olympic games, also of the (Eleusinian)
Mysteries'. But uncertainty in the following words makes it
tentative.

15. 27. 3   quod me de *Bacchide statuarum* coronis certiorem
fecisti, valde gratum.

de Bacchide, ⟨*de*⟩ (an early conjecture) and *de Bacchide* ⟨*et*⟩
(Moricca) are well enough. *de Bacchide* ⟨*et de*⟩ has perhaps a slight
advantage over the first stylistically, over the second palaeographically.

15. 29. 1   Bruti ad te epistulam misi. di boni, quanta ἀμηχανία!
cognosces cum legeris. de celebratione ludorum *Bruti* tibi
adsentior.

I doubt if Bosius' restoration of the second *Bruti* was as meritorious as he supposed. It is objectionably redundant, not to be justified by anything in Sjögren, *Comm. Tull.* pp. 160 f., and most likely a gloss on *ludorum*.

15. 29. 2 ait hic sibi *Iuliam* ferre: constitutum enim esse discidium. quaesivit ex me pater qualis esset fama. dixi nihil sane me audisse (nesciebam enim cur quaereret) nisi de ore et patre. 'sed quorsus?' inquam. at ille, filium velle. tum ego, etsi ἐβδελυττόμην, tamen negavi putare me illa esse vera.

hic is the younger Quintus, and *condicionem* is to be understood with *ferre*. Gurlitt's fantasies[1] can be disregarded.

That *Tutiam* from Lambinus' margin is right and *Iuliam* wrong is abundantly clear. TP recognized that the Tutia of 16. 2. 5 *de Tutia* (*tucia* RC) *ita putaram* is the same person—the five days' interval between the letters leaves time for Atticus' reply—and there put *Iulia* (Corradus) in their text. Would a scribe write *Iuliam* for *Tutiam*, or *Tutia* for *Iulia*? We do not need a Traube or a Lindsay to answer that. Tutia is on other grounds at least as likely a name as Julia in this context. The lady's father was objectionable and so was she. Conjectures like *de ore putri* (Schütz), *de ore et patore* [sc. *narium*] (Schmidt), *de ore et paedore* (Müller) mistake the implication of *ore*, in which I think Bosius was right to detect 'nescio quid turpe et obscenum'. See Firm. *Math.* 7. 25. 3 and *T.L.L.* s.v. *fellare* (cf. Suet. *Gramm.* 23 *usque ad infamiam oris*). *os* in 1. 18. 5 may bear a similar allusion. Even in public Cicero was not averse to dropping hints of this sort: cf. *Cael.* 78, *Post Red. in Sen.* 11, *Dom.* 25 f., 47, 83, *Har. Resp.* 11, *Sest.* 111. ἐβδελυττόμην suggests that he was thinking of something much worse than looks (Manutius etc.), impudence (Popma), or even breath. Such a person, aspiring to marriage with the younger Quintus, is not likely to have been a descendant of Venus, and no suitably discreditable father can be found for her among contemporary Caesars. True, plebeian Julii are traceable at the close of the Republic, but the *gens Tutia* is also attested, contrary to TP's belief. Republican inscriptions show it, 'merkwürdigerweise hauptsächlich bei Frauen'.[2]

---

[1] *Philol.* 1900, pp. 96–106. [2] Münzer, *RE*, s.v.

BOOK XVI

16. 1. 4.   quid ergo? ad Kal. Ian. in Pansa spes? λῆρος πολὺς in vino et in somno istorum.

Much nonsense in the slumber of those who take this to mean 'they haven't the shadow of a serious notion among them, these drowsy drinkers' (TP). Herein might seem to be included the generality of editors, who do not punctuate even by a comma (as Schütz did) after πολύς. λῆρος πολύς is an exclamation, like λῆρος in Arist. *Plut.* 23. So it is in 14. 21. 4 *sic hominem traducere ad optimates paro. λῆρος πολύς. nemo est istorum qui otium non timeat.* The right translation there is 'Rubbish!', dismissing the preceding statement, not 'a pack of fribbles!'[1] Similarly here.

How then to interpret? (*a*) Shuckburgh renders 'That's all moonshine, considering the drunken and drowsy habits of these men'. Cf. Manutius: 'se ipse accusat, qui dixerit in Pansa spem esse; cum ab iis, qui se crapulae et inertiae dediderunt, sperari nihil posset'. The causal *in* (cf. *T.L.L.* VII, 782. 47 ff.) after the exclamation appears to me incredibly harsh. (*b*) Billerbeck renders 'Possen! auf sie, diese Schlaf- und Saufhelden?' But the resumption of the construction after the exclamation is unnatural. We expect a statement, such as we get in 14. 21. 4.

I add two points on which I cannot be dogmatic. Would Cicero have used *vinum istorum* for *vinolentia istorum* or *isti vinolenti*? And, if *vino et somno istorum* is a compendious description of Pansa and his set, would he have repeated the preposition?

The text is in my judgment almost beyond defence. It is easily emended. λῆρος πολύς. *in vino et in somno istorum* ⟨*animi*⟩. Cf. 15. 12. 1 *erat animus in cursu,* ad Br. 2. 1. 3 *animum in acie esse,* Ter. *Eun.* 816 *iamdudum animus est in patinis. aū* would readily drop out after *ū*.

16. 6. 2   mehercule, mi Attice, saepe mecum 'ἡ δεῦρ' ὁδός σοι τί δύναται;'

___

[1] That is usually understood, but TP are in doubt. The aberration is responsible for some strange conjectures in 9. 18. 2, such as Reid's *in qua erat* λῆρος πολύς (*Hermath.* XII (1903), p. 259).

'*mehercule* initio sententiae Cic. numquam videtur collocasse; v. M. Heumann, Vereinzelte Beiträge (Progr. Monac. a. 1860) p. 20.' So Sjögren on 5. 16. 3. I have not been able to consult Heumann, but if he mentioned this passage editors have not listened. The rule applies not only to Cicero but to classical and pre-classical Latin generally, including Seneca, who often uses this expression. Here it is simple to supply *et*, as Lambinus did in 5. 16. 3.

16. 7. 6   reversionis has *speciosas* causas habes, iustas illas quidem et magnas; sed nulla iustior quam quod tu idem aliis litteris: 'provide, si cui quid debetur, ut sit, unde par pari respondeatur.'

Obelized, bracketed, 'emended' (*praecipuas* Lehmann), its sense distorted by Reid (*immo* before *iustas*) and by annotators who make it mean 'striking' or the like, *speciosas* is after all a harmless, necessary word, almost understood by Shuckburgh 'there you have the avowed[1] reasons for my turning back'. They are good and weighty reasons but, adds Cicero, as good as the best of them (though by no means *speciosa*) is the risk of insolvency. Cf. 6. 6. 4 *ergo haec ad populum. quid quae tecum?* To say that a reason 'looks well' does not necessarily connote that it is false or trivial.

16. 11. 1   de Sicca ita est, ut scribis; *asta ea* aegre me tenui. itaque perstringam sine ulla contumelia Siccae ⟨a⟩ut Septimiae, tantum ut sciant παῖδες παίδων, sine *vallo* Luciliano eum ex Galli Fadi filia liberos habuisse.

asta ea *MR²*, hasta ea *M²bdms*, aste *Z¹*, asturae *C*, astaga *R*, astaca *P* lucul(l)iano *Ω*

For conjectures and context see TP. I believe that *asta ea* conceals nothing more scabrous than a⟨b i⟩sta cā² (*causa*=ὑποθέσει): 'I held myself back from that theme with difficulty.' *vallo* seems insoluble. Orelli's *felle* makes the best sense. Cf. *Fam.* 12. 16. 3 *qui magis hoc Lucilio licuerit adsumere libertatis quam nobis?*

---

[1] Better 'avowable'. Mongault's translation 'voilà les raisons...qui sont pour le public' is sound, less so his note: 'les raisons qui avoient rapport aux affaires publiques, auxquelles il oppose la raison particulière' etc.

[2] *ab ista* [sc. *Septimia*, wife of Sicca] Boot. Professor Watt informs me that he has found ast ⟨ab ist⟩a cā among Housman's marginalia.

16. 11. 4   tria genera exquirendi officii esse, unum, cum deliberemus
honestum an turpe sit, *alterum, utile* an inutile, tertium, cum
haec inter se pugnare videantur.

Has not *cum* dropped out after *alterum?*

16. 13 b   rem tibi Tiro narrabit. tu quid faciendum sit videbis.
praeterea possimne propius accedere (malo enim esse in
Tusculano aut uspiam in suburbano) an etiam longius discedendum putes crebro ad me velim scribas. erit autem cotidie
cui des.

Only half-wits ask their friends to advise them every day on the
same point. Editors began to make Cicero do so in the seventeenth
century. Previously they printed thus, or nearly thus:

tu quid faciendum sit videbis, praeterea possimne propius accedere...an
etiam longius discedendum putes. crebro ad me velim scribas. erit autem
cotidie cui des.

APPENDIX

TULLIA'S FANE

Tullia died in mid February 45. Her father's plan to deify her with a temple (*fanum*) is first mentioned in a letter of March 11 (12. 18. 1). From then on until early June it is a recurrent theme in his correspondence with Atticus. Since the textual problems that arise in this connection cannot well be handled in isolation, a general account of the matter is worth attempting, with emphasis on points where commentators are at their least illuminative. I follow the dating of letters established in modern editions, mainly by the work of O. E. Schmidt and Theodor Schiche.

Some mistakes can be avoided by a clearer understanding of Cicero's motives and intentions, as they gradually emerge. Right at the start he writes that he thinks himself bound to build a shrine *quasi voto quodam et promisso* (12. 18. 1). The resolution to build it might in itself be enough to produce such a feeling, though words may easily have fallen in the first days of bereavement which seemed tantamount to a vow. He strikes the same note in 12. 23. 3 (March 19) *levatio quaedam est, si minus doloris, at officii debiti*, 12. 38a. 2 (May 7) *hoc mihi debere videor, neque levari posse nisi solvero aut videro me posse solvere*, 12. 41. 4 (May 11) *nisi hac aestate absolutum erit...scelere me liberatum non putabo*, and 12. 43. 2 (May 12) *ego me maiore religione quam quisquam fuit ullius voti obstrictum puto*. The building would salve his grief as well as his conscience: 12. 23. 3 loc. cit., 12. 41. 3 (May 11) *si me levari vis, haec est summa levatio vel, si verum scire vis, una*. In 12. 43. 2 (May 12) the MSS. have *quod scies recte mihi* (om. Δ) *illam rem fore levamento bene facis cum* (*quom* O, *tum* cod. Faerni) *id esse* (*esset* bmsO[2]), *mihi crede perinde ut existimare tu non potes*, where *scribis* (Z[1], Manutius) for *scies*, which may have come from a neighbouring *scies*, is practically certain. On *recte*, I agree with Lattmann[1] in rejecting *reri te* (Manutius), *rere* (Madvig, omitting *scies*), and *existimare te* (Wesenberg), on the ground that, after reading Cicero's letters on the subject,[2] Atticus

---

[1] *Philol.* 1890, pp. 187–9.
[2] But not the one Lattmann cites, 12. 41; compare the dates.

might have written *credo*, but not *reor* or *existimo*. Lambinus' *certe* is inadequate. But *recte* can hardly stand, and I incline to read *quod scribis scire te mihi illam rem fore levamento, bene facis; quin* (Lattmann) *id esse* et sqq.

A consideration additional to these of sentiment soon comes into view. Since Tullia's death life in Rome had become distasteful to Cicero (12. 28. 2 of March 24 *nunc plane nec ego victum nec vitam illam colere possum*). The idea of giving up his town house appears as early as March 19 (12. 23. 1): *meis litteris respondisti, ut de foro et de curia. sed domus est, ut ais, forum. quid ipsa domo mihi opus est carenti foro?* This looks back to 12. 21. 5 *quod me in forum vocas, eo vocas unde etiam bonis meis rebus fugiebam. quid enim mihi foro sine iudiciis, sine curia* et sqq. Atticus will have answered 'You need not go into the forum. Your own house will be forum and senate house' (i.e. 'As long as you are in the capital, receiving visitors, you will escape criticism even if you don't appear in public'). Cicero, following perhaps his own thoughts rather than his correspondent's, rejoins 'Why keep a town house at all, if I don't go out in public?' But if the town house were abandoned, it would be convenient to possess a property nearer to Rome than Tusculum or Astura. Hence there takes shape a project to buy a suburban estate (*horti*), which might contain both a temple for Tullia and a residence for Cicero.

In three passages this idea is implied by the word ἐγγήραμα, a noun found only once elsewhere, in Plutarch, *Cato Maior*, 24 ὥσπερ Διονύσιόν τις ἔπεισε κάλλιστον ἐντάφιον ἡγεῖσθαι τὴν τυραννίδα, κάλλιστον αὐτὸς ἐγγήραμα τὴν πολιτείαν ποιησάμενος. I suspect that Cato's saying was originally to the effect that a free state, *respublica*, is the best place to grow old in, though in the Plutarchian context one has to understand 'public life is the best way of spending an old age'. Be that as it may, the root sense of ἐγγήραμα must be something, place or occupation, in which one grows old, ἐγγηρᾷ, as for example ἐντρύφημα is something in which one takes delight, ἐντρυφᾷ.

On March 21, with reference to the purchase of *horti*, Cicero ends his letter (12. 25) thus: *mihi crede, una me causa movet, in qua scio me* τετυφῶσθαι. *sed, ut facis, obsequere huic errori meo. nam quod scribis* ἐγγήραμα, *actum iam de isto est: alia magis quaero*. The letter of Atticus which Cicero is answering will have been written in reply to

12. 23 of March 19. Taking up Cicero's remark that his house on the Palatine might as well be given up, Atticus must have suggested that the *horti* which Cicero was proposing to buy (12. 23. 3) might serve as an ἐγγήραμα, a retreat for his old age. For the moment Cicero disclaims any such interest. He has only one motive (*causa*), the shrine. As for his old age and where to spend it, all concern for that is over: *longum illud tempus cum non ero magis me movet quam hoc exiguum, quod mihi tamen nimium longum videtur* (12. 18. 1 of March 11). Victorius' explanation of ἐγγήραμα is wholly acceptable: 'locum in quo senectus commode transigi possit et qui sit requies et oblectamentum eius aetatis'.

A very different interpretation prevails. It is based on the second occurrence of ἐγγήραμα, in 12. 29. 2 (March 25): ǀvel tu illud ἐγγήραμα, *quemadmodum scripsisti, vel ἐντάφιον putato.* Corradus saw that this alludes to Cato the Elder's remark, which as understood, rightly or wrongly, by Plutarch meant that public service was the best employment for old age, just as despotism in Dionysius' opinion made the best winding-sheet (ἐντάφιον). Hence Atticus is supposed to have advised 'dying in harness' as an active politician. This is well enough for TP, but how did it escape Corradus or even Boot that the advice would have been absurd in the existing state of politics, that the passage in 12. 25 relates only to the purchase of *horti*, and that ἐγγήραμα there is unlikely to mean something (*respublica*) which it cannot possibly mean in 12. 29. 2, where *illud* must be the proposed purchase ('call it a retreat for old age, as you have put it, or a shroud')? Of course Cato's phrase was in mind, but only for the sake of the contrast between ἐγγήραμα and ἐντάφιον. The *horti* will be for dying in rather than for living in. This is no less certainly, and perhaps yet more obviously, the sense of ἐγγήραμα in 12. 44. 2.[1]

As time went on Cicero came more and more to look on the *horti* as an ἐγγήραμα rather than as an ἐντάφιον. By May 23 (13. 1. 2) he is writing that there is no kind of property he would like better, chiefly of course (*scilicet*) for the purpose of the shrine, but also *ad καταβίωσιν maestitiamque minuendam.* Jac. Gronovius explains *ad καταβίωσιν* as 'ad decursum reliquum vitae' ('life's downward slope', TP, 'decline of life', Liddell–Scott–Jones). Probably however it means merely 'for passing my life', as in Diod. 18. 52. 3 μίαν

[1] See below, p. 94.

λαβόντα πόλιν εἰς καταβίωσιν τὴν ἡσυχίαν ἄγειν and App. *B.C.* 4. 16 ἐπανελθόντων ἀφανὴς καταβίωσις.[1] Five days later the residential aspect is uppermost: 13. 31. 4 *nihil enim aliud reperio ubi et in foro non sim et tecum esse possim.*

Where to build the shrine? The site first suggested (12. 19. 1 of March 14) is Cicero's seaside villa at Astura, but that is immediately put aside. Already he thinks of the suburbs: *cogito interdum trans Tiberim hortos aliquos parare, et quidem ob hanc causam maxime.*[2] *nihil enim video quod tam celebre esse possit. sed quos, coram videbimus.* That *celebritas* was a capital point appears from several passages, one of which (13. 22. 4) has caused trouble: *lucum hominibus non sane probo quod est desertior: sed habet* ἐυλογίαν. Wesenberg's obelus and the various substitutes for *hominibus* proposed by Schütz, Fr. Schmidt, and Reid are needless. In the case of a mortal like Tullia the principal purpose of a fane was to keep alive the memory of the dead, to which a secluded site must be adverse. None the less a sacred grove had ἐυλογίαν. Boot might have been less tempted by ἐυωνίαν (Schütz) and TP by ἐυαγίαν if Cicero's use of ἐύλογος in 13. 5, 13. 6a, 13. 7 and 14. 22. 2 had been clearly understood. He uses this adjective of a hypothesis which is likely because it fits facts already known. Here he means that a grove, despite the disadvantage of seclusion, 'has plausibility' because it comports with ἀποθέωσις; such being the natural habitat of divinities. In 12. 12. 1 of March 16 he remarks that the *insula Arpinas* (an island, presumably wooded, in the Fibrinus) might provide *germanam* ἀποθέωσιν, but fears that its out of the way situation (ἐκτοπισμός) would make it seem less honourable to the dead.

'Gardens' then, but what 'gardens'? On March 17 three candidates come into view: *venales certe sunt Drusi, fortasse et Lamiani et Cassiani.* Of the last there is no further mention. Lamia was away[3] (12. 22. 3), and the *Lamiani* are presently dropped as impracticable (12. 29. 2). To postpone Drusus for a moment, two other possible

---

[1] Liddell–Scott–Jones loosely render 'residence' in both passages.

[2] I put a full stop instead of the usual colon. *hanc causam* is not 'the following reason', but 'this reason', i.e. the shrine.

[3] This is rather curious, as L. Aelius Lamia seems to have been aedile of the plebs in 45 (see Broughton). It is possible of course that he is not the man. The MSS. present us with a senator called C. Lamia in *Q. Fr.* 2. 11. 2, but *L.* is usually read.

vendors can be briefly dismissed. L. Aurelius Cotta (consul in 65) had property near Ostia, with the advantage of *celebritas*; but it was small, with a mean little villa (12. 23. 3, 27. 1), and so after March 23 no more is heard of it. A place belonging to Damasippus, probably the connoisseur of Hor. *Sat.* 2. 3, crops up in two letters (12. 29. 2, 33. 1). In the second (of March 26) Atticus is asked to approach him, but nothing came of it.

The two *horti* most seriously considered during March were the *Drusiani* and the *Siliani* (the latter first mentioned on the 18th, 12. 22. 3). The owner of the former will have been M. Livius Drusus Claudianus, father of Livia Augusta, whom Cicero successfully defended in 54. Silius' identity is not so immediately clear. It is usual to distinguish, as does Münzer, between P. Silius,[1] propraetor of Bithynia in 50, and A. Silius, owner of these 'gardens'; but the evidence wilts under inspection. In all but two of the numerous references to the 'gardens' their owner appears as simply 'Silius'. Editors present the praenomen A. in 12. 24 (March 20), which begins in their texts *bene fecit A. Silius qui transegerit. neque enim ei deesse volebam et quid possem timebam*, and in 12. 26. 1 *Sicca, ut scribit, etiamsi nihil confecerit cum A. Silio* et sqq. As Gronovius and others since have remarked, it does not look as though the man named in the first passage was the owner of the *horti*. Evidently he had settled some dispute in which he had wanted Cicero's assistance, but nothing is heard of it elsewhere.[2] His name in the MSS. appears as *asyllius* or (in RP) *asilius*. It is far from certain that this represents *A. Silius* (*Asinius*[3] would be pretty well as close), but if it does the praenomen is in all probability used to distinguish him from the owner of the *horti*. In the second passage the MSS. offer the strange reading *cum agidio*. How this arose from *cum Silio* (cf. 12. 32. 1 *nam cum Silio non video confici posse*) I do not pretend to say,[4] but it is scant excuse for putting a superfluous and improbable praenomen in the text, on which to base prosopographical conclusions.

---

[1] Münzer (*RE*, III A, 72) points out that we have no right to give him the cognomen Nerva, though he may have been the father of P. Silius Nerva, consul in 20 B.C.

[2] This of course, is not conclusive. Cicero did give some legal assistance to a Silius about a year later (15. 23, 24).

[3] Not Pollio, who was in Spain.

[4] Perhaps the first stage was *cum scilio* (so in the preceding letter, 12. 25. 1).

Once this praenomen is eliminated nothing separates the proprietor of the *horti* from the praetorius, also called simply by his
nomen in the Atticus correspondence (6. 1. 13 and 7. 1. 8 for certain).
Cicero knew him (cf. the recommendatory letters, *Fam.* 13. 61–5),
as did Atticus (7. 1. 8; cf. 12. 18a. 2). And the owner of these
desirable 'gardens' was likely to be a person of rank, like Drusus,
Cotta, Clodia,[1] even Lamia, not a nobody. But as it happens the
identification can be confirmed by a piece of positive evidence. Of
Silius' 'gardens' Cicero writes in 12. 31. 2 (March 29) *quaeris a me*
quod summum pretium constituam et quantum anteire istos hortos
Drusi. accessi numquam; Coponianam villam et veterem ⟨et⟩ non
magnam novi, silvam nobilem. The Coponian villa is certainly not a
separate property. As Boot says, it is never mentioned again, and
this passage is concerned only with the *Siliani* and *Drusiani*. If
quantum anteire istos hortos Drusi meant '[you ask me] how much
superior do I think those grounds of Drusus' (TP, sim. Shuckburgh), what follows would refer to Drusus' gardens. But Cicero
did not write *istos* to exercise his fingers, and Atticus is not likely to
have forgotten 12. 25. 2 *Drusianis vero hortis multo antepono*
[*hortos Silii*], *neque sunt umquam comparati.* With this advantage he
will have construed correctly: 'you ask me how far I put those
"gardens" [of Silius] ahead of Drusus' [in price]'. How anyone who
did so should fail to see that the *Villa Coponiana* belonged to Silius'
estate, not that of Drusus, is hard to understand; but so was it with
Boot. Now Velleius (2. 83) mentions that Coponius, *vir e praetoriis*
gravissimus (i.e. C. Coponius, praetor in 49), was P. Silius' father-in-
law. Hence the *villa Coponiana.* Coponius was still living, but Silius
may have acquired the property as his wife's dowry, or possibly
Coponius, an active Pompeian, had lost it by confiscation.[2]

Both these *horti* lay beyond the Tiber at some distance from
Rome. That is implied in 12. 44. 2[3] and, for the *Siliani*, in 12. 27. 1,
where Cotta's property *in Ostiensi* is said to be situated *ultra*
[*Silianam villam*].

Besides their intrinsic superiority to the *Drusiani*, the *Siliani* were
recommended by the prospect that their proprietor, presumably a

[1] See below, p. 95.
[2] This disposes of Wesenberg's *Silianam* for *silvam.*
[3] See below, p. 94.

wealthy man, would not insist on immediate payment: 12. 22. 3 *et is* (so rightly Lipsius for *iis*) *usuris facillime sustentabitur.* Drusus on the other hand was anxious to sell (ibid. *cupit vendere,* 12. 37. 2 *certe vendere vult*), but he would want cash down. Moreover, he was asking too much: 12. 23. 3 (March 19) *de Drusi hortis, quanti licuisse tu scribis, id ego audieram et, ut opinor, heri ad te scripseram. sed quanti quanti, bene emitur quod necesse est,* 12. 33. 1 (March 26) *si et Silius is fuerit quem tu putas nec Drusus facilem se praebuerit,* 12. 31. 2 (March 29) *si venalis non haberet [Silius], transirem ad Drusum vel tanti quanti Egnatius*[1] *illum velle tibi dixit,* 12. 38a. 2 (May 7) *de Drusi hortis, quamvis ab iis abhorreas, ut scribis, tamen eo confugiam, nisi quid inveneris,* 12. 41. 3 (May 11) *si Silius nolet, Drusus aget iniuste,* 13. 26. 1 (May 14) *quod si neutrum, metuo ne turbem et irruam in Drusum.* I have quoted these passages partly to pave the way for the reformation of 12. 37. 2 (May 4) *si nihil erit, etsi tu meam stultitiam consuesti ferre, eo tamen progrediar ut stomachere. Drusus enim certe vendere vult. si ergo aliud erit, non mea erit culpa nisi emero. qua in re ne labar, quaeso, provide.* Neither Lehmann's defence of this,[2] with which most modern editors are satisfied, nor the conjectures of Graevius (*si ergo aliud non erit, mea erit culpa nisi emero*) and J. F. Gronovius (*si ergo nihil aliud erit, non mea erit culpa nisi emero*) meet the case. The passages quoted above, especially 12. 38a. 2 and 13. 26. 1, point plainly to *si ergo aliud ⟨de⟩erit, non mea erit culpa si emero.* It will not be Cicero's fault if he is forced to buy from Drusus for lack of an alternative. In fact he always knew that the Drusus property was a bad bargain, and his reiterated threats to commit the imprudence of buying it were clearly meant as a spur to Atticus, of whose coolness towards the whole project he was well aware.[3] The last reference to them is that of May 14. On the 13th (12. 44. 2) comes the odd phrase *si nihil fiet, aut Druso ludus est suggerendus aut utendum Tusculano. ludum suggerere* occurs nowhere else, and is supposed to be an equivalent of *ludos facere (ludificari).* But nothing suggests that Drusus was to be or could be 'bam-

---

[1] Egnatius acted as intermediary in negotiations with Drusus, as did Sicca (as well as Atticus) in those with Silius.

[2] *Quaest. Tull.* pp. 43 f.

[3] Cf. for example 12. 43. 2 *tibi. . .quem id non ita valde probare arbitrer.* But statements that Atticus deliberately created difficulties or that he did exactly nothing lie outside the evidence.

'boozled', neither does this interpretation suit the usual force of *suggerere*. I think the meaning is 'we must give Drusus a game', i.e. take things up ('play ball') with him.

With Silius, on the other hand, Cicero meant business. Negotiations proceeded during March and perhaps afterwards through Atticus and Sicca. But there was always a doubt whether Silius really wanted to sell, and in the end he decided against it, for a reason or on an excuse connected with his son (12. 31. 1). Yet sporadic references in May and June (12. 52, 13. 5. 1, 13. 7. 1) suggest that the possibility may not have been entirely given up even then.

Cicero spent April with Atticus in his villa near Nomentum, so the correspondence lapses after March 30, to be resumed on May 1 or 2 with 12. 35. In this he raises a point which had just occurred to him. A sumptuary law existed by which expense on a tomb (*monumentum*) in excess of a certain limit entailed a fine equal to the amount of the excess. This, he says, would not worry him, were it not that in any case he wished the building to be called a shrine (*fanum*) and nothing else; *quod si volumus, vereor ne adsequi non possimus nisi mutato loco*. With this passage must be compared the first paragraph of the next letter, 12. 36 (May 3):

Fanum fieri volo, neque hoc mihi erui potest. sepulcri similitudinem effugere non tam propter poenam legis studeo quam ut maxime adsequar ἀποθέωσιν. quod poteram si in ipsa villa facerem; sed, ut saepe locuti sumus, commutationes dominorum reformido. in agro ubicumque fecero, mihi videor adsequi posse ut posteritas habeat religionem...sin tibi res, si locus, si institutum placet, lege quaeso, legem, mihique eam mitte. si quid in mentem veniet, quomodo eam effugere possimus, utemur.

All commentators err here, though not all so extravagantly as TP. How much of the following explanation is original I leave the reader to discover for himself if he cares.

First the words *si res, si locus, si institutum placet*. *res* cannot be the whole scheme of the shrine, which was not in debate (Atticus did not much approve of it, as Cicero well knew), and must refer to a particular project of purchase discussed in Atticus' villa. *locus* is the site, *institutum* probably the building plan. The allusion can only be to the *horti* of Scapula in the Campus Vaticanus (13. 33a. 1), first mentioned specifically in the following letter (12. 37. 2). He could build for Tullia either inside the house precincts (*villa*) or on the surrounding land. A building inside the villa might be disturbed by subsequent owners who would find it in their way. A building *in agro*[1] would not be in danger of such interference, but as the area contained many *monumenta*[2] it would not be easy to retain there the distinctive character of a *fanum*. But a *fanum* is what Cicero wants, so he may have to look elsewhere (*quod vereor ne adsequi non possimus nisi mutato loco*). As for the law, which applied to a *monumentum* but not a *fanum*, he would not much care about it if he wanted the former; but in fact he wants the latter, and the law is an additional reason for wanting it. All the same, if (*sin*), despite the difficulties attaching to the Scapulan *horti*, Atticus does on the whole approve of them, the law must be looked into—for if the building was to be *in agro*, it might be regarded as *a monumentum* and so within the scope of the law, which must be circumvented if possible.[3]

In fact, the Scapulan property remained in favour. Its owner, possibly the T. Quinctius Scapula who led a defection of Caesarian troops in Baetica after Thapsus (*Fam.* 9. 13. 1, Dio 43. 29), had recently died, and his estate awaited distribution between four heirs. Of these most is heard of one Otho, who may or may not have been the author of the Lex Roscia. Cicero's aim was to have the 'gardens' put up to auction so that outside bidders would get a chance (12. 38a. 2, 39. 4 etc.), and Atticus is asked to do his utmost to this end. He seems to have succeeded, but on July 9, just before the auction took place, Cicero heard privately that Caesar's architectural plans would involve the Campus Vaticanus (13. 33a. 1). That virtually put an end to the whole *fanum* project, though a solitary reference in 15. 15. 3 (13 June 44) shows that even a year later it had not been openly abandoned.

A textual point arises in 13. 3. 1 *de Crispo et Mustela videbis, et velim scire quae sit pars duorum* (*istorum* ds), on which Reid[4] has 'Some of the earlier editors noted a difficulty about *duorum*, viz. that it is not used to signify "the two" or "these two" of persons already mentioned. I have never seen a precise parallel.' Comparing Ov.

---

[1] Cf. 13. 52. 1 *castra in agro: villa defensa est.*

[2] So Popma and others. Whether this was really the difficulty I am not sure, but some difficulty there evidently was.

[3] That Cicero was afraid of looking like a tax evader if he built a *fanum* is a figment of TP's.   [4] *Hermath.* x (1899), p. 331.

Fast. 2. 629 *et soror et Procne Tereusque duabus iniquus*, ibid. 3. 868 *ille vehit per freta longa duos*, Mart. 7. 38. 3 *fera monstra duorum* (*Cyclopis et Scyllae*), Cato ap. Gell. 14. 2. 26 *si quis quid alter ab altero peterent...quod duo res gessissent, uti testes non interessent* et sqq. I do not think it necessary (despite the absence of Ciceronian parallels) to substitute *eorum* (Ernesti) or *duorum horum* (Orelli).

Of the buildings in these *horti* we hear something in 13. 29. 1. The villa was unattractive (*insulsitatem bene noram*); the area, which included a *lucus*, may have been in the region of 1000 *iugera* (13. 31. 4). There were two capital advantages, *celebritas* and proximity to the city: 12. 37. 2 *maxima est in Scapulae celebritas, propinquitas praeterea urbis* (so Fr. Schmidt for *ubi sis*), *ne totum diem in villa*. People who have no notion what Cicero is talking about here can afford to reject Manutius' *villa* in favour of *villam* in the MSS. He intended to reside in these *horti*: 13. 31. 4 *nihil enim aliud reperio ubi et in foro non sim et tecum esse possim*. The villa is not that at Tusculum, mentioned earlier in the paragraph, but the house in the *horti*; and the implied comparison is with the more distant *horti* of Silius and Drusus. From the Campus Vaticanus he could be at Atticus' *domus* on the Quirinal in half an hour. No need there to sit all day in the villa. Similarly in another commentator's quagmire 12. 44. 2 *mihi vero et locum quem opto ad id quod volumus dederis et praeterea* ἐγγήραμα. *nam illa Sili et Drusi non satis* οἰκοδεσποτικὰ *mihi videntur. quid enim? sedere totos dies in villa? ista igitur malim, primum Othonis, deinde Clodiae*: '[If you get me Otho's place] you will give me both the site I want [for the shrine] and an "old man's home" as well. Those places of Silius and Drusus don't seem to me quite the thing for the master of the house. One doesn't want to spend all one's days in a villa [like a *vilicus*].'

Besides the 'gardens' of Scapula, three other new sites were envisaged at this period. 12. 37. 2 (May 4): *de fano, si nihil mihi hortorum invenis, ⟨qui⟩ quidem tibi inveniendi sunt si me tanti facis quanti certe facis, valde probo rationem tuam de Tusculano. quamvis prudens ad cogitandum sis, sicut es, tamen, nisi magnae curae tibi esset ut ego consequerer id quod magnopere vellem, numquam ea res tibi tam belle in mentem venire potuisset. sed nescio quo pacto celebritatem requiro; itaque hortos mihi conficias necesse est.* Evidently, Cicero's estate at Tusculum had been mooted by Atticus in a letter just received (not while they were together in April), and this is Cicero's first reaction. A week later (12. 41. 3) he is willing to acquiesce if Atticus is in favour of this site (*ut significasti quibusdam litteris*), and on the 12th he asks him to consider it along with other possibilities (12. 43. 3). After two further mentions, as a *pis aller*, on the 13th (12. 44. 2) and 14th (13. 26. 1), it drops out.

In 12. 38a. 2 (May 7) comes a passing reference to *ille locus Publicianus qui est Treboni et Cusini*; but this was an empty site and so quite unsuitable (*nullo pacto probo*). None the less on May 11 (12. 41. 3) it is reckoned as a possibility if the other *horti* are unobtainable, and on the 12th Atticus is asked to see about it (12. 43. 2), though the owners are away. Presumably the place had belonged to a Publicius, possibly to M. Publicius who was *legatus pro praetore* to Cn. Pompeius the younger in 46.[1] At any rate, the names of the existing owners suggest that he was an expropriated Pompeian. Trebonius needs no introduction, Cusinius will be M. Cusinius, praetor in 44, whom Antony named governor of Sicily. Rebilus, mentioned as a third owner in 12. 41. 3, was doubtless the one-day consul of 45. Probably all three were at this time with Caesar in Spain.

But the estate which, next to Scapula's, now chiefly interested Cicero belonged to a Clodia. It first occurs in 12. 38a. 2 (May 7): *Clodiae sane placent, sed non puto esse venales*, and on four successive days (May 10–13) is named as second in attractiveness only to the *Scapulani*. On May 16, as difficulties with Scapula's heirs accumulated, Cicero inclined towards the Clodian property, though still preferring the other (12. 47). But Clodia was away from Rome (12. 42. 1, 47. 2, 52. 2), and doubt about her willingness to sell persisted (12. 52. 2). The last reference comes in 13. 29. 2 (May 27):[2] *Clodiam igitur, a qua ipsa ob eam causam sperare videor quod et multo minoris sunt* et sqq. The force of *ipsa* here is usually missed: Cicero hopes to buy from Clodia directly, without having to bid at an auction.

These 'gardens' then were much cheaper than the *Scapulani*, and, like them, lay very near Rome (12. 44. 2). Their owner was probably one of P. Clodius Pulcher's three sisters, which one cannot certainly

---

[1] Grueber, *Coins etc.* II. 364 f.
[2] Unless 14. 8. 1 (April 44) *Clodia quid egerit scribas ad me velim* is one.

be determined; but I think 12. 52. 2 (May 21) is a pointer: *tu mihi aut Scapulanos aut Clodianos efficias necesse est. sed nescio quid videris dubitare de Clodia; utrum quando veniat an sintne venales? sed quid est, quod audio Spintherem fecisse divortium?* The last sentence has not hitherto been thought to have any connection with what precedes, but perhaps it is not unreasonable to suggest that Spinther's divorce was somehow linked with Clodia in the writer's mind. Spinther (P. Cornelius Lentulus Spinther, son of the consul of 57) was married to a Metella (13. 7. 1) of uncertain provenance. The hypothesis occurs that she was the daughter of Q. Metellus Celer and the celebrated Quadrantaria—a worthy daughter, 'berüchtigt durch seine Sittenlosigkeit'.[1] So in this Clodia I incline to see the βοῶπις of the second book of the Letters and Lentulus Spinther's mother-in-law.[2] In 12. 40. 4 of May 9, two days after the first mention of Clodia's 'gardens', comes a sentence usually held corrupt. Cicero is urging Atticus to get the Scapulan 'gardens' put up for auction, in which case *vincemus facultates Othonis nostra cupiditate. nam quod ad me de Lentulo scribis, non est in eo. Faberiana modo res certa sit tuque enitare, quod facis, quod volumus consequemur.* The words *non est in eo,* obelized by Purser and variously altered by conjecture, are defensible Latin in the sense 'it does not depend on him'. In such expressions *esse* has a variety of subjects (*totum, omnia, multum, aliquid, id* and many more: see Müller, pp. xlix ff.), or the subject may be a dependent clause as in Quint. *Inst.* 6. 1. 10 *in epilogo vero est, qualem animum iudex in consilium ferat.* In *Dom.* 11 it is *res: res erat non in opinione dubia, sed in praesenti atque ante oculos proposito periculo.* Here it is *res*, understood (see Sjögren on 7. 8. 5 *movet*, though I do not follow him in that passage). Now if the Lentulus of 12. 40. 4 is Cicero's infant grandson[3] this sense is no sense at all. But what if he is, not 'some unknown Lentulus (of whom we do not hear elsewhere) who was anxious to buy the *horti* of Scapula' (TP), but Lentulus Spinther (called 'Lentulus' in 13. 7. 1), Clodia's son-in-law?[4] Atticus had just replied to 12. 38a, where Cicero remarks tha

---

[1] *RE*, iii. 1235 f.

[2] Another, but weaker, link could be forged out of 9. 6. 3, where a Clodia appears as mother-in-law of L. Metellus, tribune in 49.

[3] He would probably have been called *Lentulus puer* as in 12. 28. 3 (I do not forget 12. 30. 1).

[4] This suggestion is not new, only the reasons for it.

he likes the idea of Clodia's 'gardens' but thinks they are not for sale. If Atticus, along with some deprecation of the Scapulan purchase as expensive and difficult to arrange, had suggested that Lentulus Spinther, a friend and the son of a friend, could help in the Clodian matter, Cicero's answer is intelligible as it stands in the MSS.: 'My eagerness will offset Otho's wealth. As for what you say about Lentulus, it [i.e. Clodia's selling] doesn't rest with him.' Let Atticus concentrate on the *Scapulani* and all will turn out well.

In 56 Clodia possessed *horti* on the Tiber, probably opposite the Campus Martius: *Cael.* 36 *hortos ad Tiberim diligenter eo loco parasti, quo omnis iuventus natandi causa venit.*[1] The situation fits, and there is piquancy in the possibility that this *Zaubergarten* might have become Cicero's ἐγγήραμα.

Cicero's capacity to pay for his plans, which depended mainly on the recovery of a loan from Caesar's secretary Faberius, is a separate topic on which I am content to refer to O. E. Schmidt's discussion[2] with a few textual comments.

12. 23. 3   nec tamen ista pretia hortorum pertimueris. nec mihi argento iam nec veste opus est nec *quibusdam* amoenis locis; hoc opus est.

quibusdam can hardly stand. It must mean, as TP without confidence explain, that Cicero had no need of some of his villas [but had need of others]. Apart from the oddity of the Latin (*tot* would be natural), he is here thinking rhetorically, not practically, and is no more likely to make reservations about the villas than about the plate and coverlets. Pluygers' imaginary fragment of Lucilius, *nec mihi tam argento nec veste opus est neque bubus* (followed by *quam amoenis locis*) may be 'very ingenious, and worthy of that acute scholar', but *amoenis locis* doubtless refers to villas: 16. 3. 4 *in praediolis nostris et belle aedificatis et satis amoenis* (cf. *Fam.* 7. 20. 2). Castiglioni's *quibus gaudebam* makes excellent sense, but *quibus quondam* (*qđa*: sc. *opus erat*) is a more likely origin.

[1] G. Lugli, who assumes that these are the gardens which Cicero wished to buy, suggests that they occupied the site of the Villa Farnese: *Mélanges de l'école française de Rome*, 1938, pp. 25–7.
[2] *Briefwechsel*, pp. 289–307.

12. 25. 1   reliquae pecuniae vel usuram Silio pendemus, dum a
Faberio vel *cum* aliquo qui Faberio debet repraesentabimus.

velim usuram...pendamus *Schmidt,* vel *del. Kayser*   cum] ab *Pius*

repraesentabimus is often taken 'until I get cash from Faberius'.
So TP who, on 12. 31. 1, remark that '*repraesentare* generally means
"to pay ready money for a debt due some time hence": in these
letters it more frequently means "to receive ready money"'. So
Schmidt,[1] 'diskontieren'. It is nowhere in Cicero necessary to
accept this meaning,[2] and here Budaeus' interpretation is clearly
right, 'until we can pay cash down'. *a*='at the expense of' is
normal. *cum* is best deleted—possibly it arose from a repetition of
dum.

12. 31. 1   Silium mutasse sententiam Sicca mirabatur. equidem
magis miror quod, cum in filium causam conferret, quae mihi
non iniusta videtur—habet enim quale⟨m⟩ vult—ais te putare,
si addiderimus aliud a quo *refugiat* cum ab ipso id fuerit destinatum, venditurum.

fuerit *C*: fieret *ΔO*

Here, as often in Cicero's references to business matters, ignorance
of the facts imposes caution. An explicable text can be had from a
slight change, of *refugiat* to *refugit.* This is to presuppose that Silius
at an earlier stage had offered to take some property of Cicero's in
part exchange for his *horti* (*destinatum* in this context must be given
its business sense), but had later withdrawn the offer. Atticus had
now expressed the view that Silius might be willing to sell if this
item were added to the purchase price. This Cicero finds inconsistent
with Silius' earlier conduct.

13. 1. 2   de pecunia vero video a te omnem diligentiam adhiberi vel
potius iam adhibitam esse. *quod si* efficis, a te hortos habebo.

quod si *C*: om. *Ω*   efficis enim a te *RP*, efficis a te enim *O*

I agree with Schmidt that *quod si* is probably a conjecture, but
prefer it to his *et sicunde* (for *efficis*). *quam si* would be more idiomatic, however: cf. Plaut. *Bacch.* 233 *unde aurum ecficiam amanti
erili filio.*

[1] P. 290.
[2] Nor in *Dig.* 35. 1. 36, quoted by Schmidt *exempli gratia.*

ADDENDA

9. 8. 1   de L. Torquato quod quaeris, non modo Lucius sed etiam
Aulus profectus est, alter multos.

Castiglioni's supplement *alter paucos ante dies* leaves nothing to
be desired except a homoeoteleuton. Read *alter multos ⟨ante dies,
alter paucos⟩*.

9. 15. 3   *sed tu,* omnia qui consilia differebas in id tempus cum
sciremus quae Brundisi acta essent, scimus nempe; haeremus
nihilo minus.

qui om. ms

Sjögren's 'distinguendi medela' can be examined in his text, or
Moricca's. The choice really lies between an anacoluthon and a small
supplement, such as *sed ⟨heus⟩ tu* (Schmidt) or *sed ⟨quid⟩ tu* (Purser).
I have no quarrel with the latter (cf. *Phil.* 8. 12 *sed quaeso, Calene,
quid tu?*), but a slight preference for *sed tu ⟨quid⟩*—the nearer *quia*
stood to *qui* the easier its disappearance. Cf. 15. 29. 2 *sed tu quid ais?*

9. 17. 2   ad me enim ipse Tiro ita scripsit ut verear quid agat.
qui autem veniunt *ni id modo* nuntiant.

ni (mihi *s*) id modo *Mdms,* ni admodo *O,* in id modo *bZ^b,* inni admodo *Z^l,*
inanio *R,* indumodo *codd. Graevii*

inde (*inde* κινδυνωδῶς Bosius), κινδυνώδη (Ernesti) and *admodum*
(*inania admodum* Lambinus) may all be right: *qui autem veniunt inde,*
κινδυνώδη *admodum nuntiant. inde* κινδυνώδη in Roman letters,
compressed perhaps into *indunode,* will have started the trouble.
Most editors see the merit of κινδυνώδη (cf. 13. 19. 1 *tu ἀκίνδυνα
esse scribis*), to which Sjögren prefers Malaespina's far less apt *inania*
(*qui autem veniunt, inania admodum nuntiant*).

9. 19. 1   vide ipse Formiis universos, neque mehercule *numquam*
homines putavi; et noram omnes, sed numquam uno loco
videram.

numquam (nun-) ΔOR, non quam M² in marg., unquam P

Whether or not Cicero could have written the double negative, as Sjögren thought possible on the strength of Pl. *Pseud.* 136 and *Verr.* 2. 60, the best thing to do with the first *numquam* is to bracket it as a copyist's anticipation of the second. So, and only so, *et. . .videram* acquires point. Cicero thought the Caesarians less than human *after* seeing them all together at Formiae. True, he already knew them as individuals, but he had never before seen them collected in one place—and so had not quite realised their enormity.

10. 16. 2　consilium nostrum spero vacuum periculo fore; nam et dissimulavimus *et*, ut opinor, acerrime adservabimur.

non (Madvig) is usually added before *acerrime*. Better, *nec, ut opinor*. . . . For *et. . .nec* see Kühner–Stegmann II, p. 49.

11. 1. 2　huius pecuniae permutatione fidem nostram facile tuebere; quam quidem ego nisi expeditam relinquere putassem credens ei cui tu scis iam pridem *minime* credere, commoratus essem paulisper nec domesticas res impeditas reliquissem.

ei is usually supposed to be Terentia's steward Philotimus; I take it to mean Terentia herself.

Lehmann's addition *credere ⟨me debere⟩* makes sense, but that can be done more neatly by writing *nimium me* for *minime*.

11. 6. 2　minus sermonis subissem, minus accepissem doloris, ipsum hoc me non angeret. Brundisi iacere in omnis partis est molestum. propius accedere, ut suades, quo modo sine lictoribus, quos populus dedit, possum?

So editors. But *ipsum hoc* ('quod me nunc angit, erroris videlicet mei recordatio', Manutius) is far from clear. Best take it, with a colon after *angeret*, as anticipating the dilemma.

11. 15. 1　quoniam iustas causas adfers quod te hoc tempore videre non possim, quaeso, quid sit mihi faciendum.

'Ante vel post *quaeso* add. *vide* aut *cogita* alii, sed *scribe* cogitatione addendum; cfr. x. 13, 3 ', Sjögren. 10. 13. 3 begins *tu, quaeso, si quid in Hispaniis*, which suggests that *tu* should be added after *possim*—though *iam* might have fallen out even more easily. *scribe* cannot be supplied from nothing at all.

12. 1. 1   atque utinam continuo ad complexum meae Tulliae, ad
osculum Atticae *possim* currere!

Read *possem*. Cicero, writing from Arpinum, has explained that
he is to stop the night at Anagnia, spend the next two nights at
Tusculum, and keep an appointment in Rome (with his brother)
on the day following. The day after that is assigned to Axius, the
next to Atticus (§2). So he cannot run straight to Tullia and Attica;
but he wishes he could.

12. 38*a*. 2   κύρσας mihi sic placuit ut cetera Antisthenis, hominis
acuti magis quam eruditi.

κγρcαc MdmOPZ⁽ᵇ⁾: κιρσας R: κύρβας Z^β

Bosius says in his commentary that his codices (which should
include *Z*) had κύρσας, but κύρβας is his note in Parisinus 8538A.
His conjecture Κῦρος δ, ε (i.e. δ', ε') rests on Diogenes Laertius'
account of Antisthenes' works (6. 1. 16), which were arranged in
ten τόμοι. Two dialogues entitled Κῦρος were included in the fourth
and fifth of these (cf. *Athen.* 5. 220b ἐν θατέρῳ τῶν Κύρων), and no
one seems to have found any difficulty in believing with Bosius that
these are here referred to as 'Cyrus 4 and 5'. Two dialogues called
'Alcibiades' are attributed to Plato and form part of his fourth
Tetralogy. Could either of them on that account be called 'Alcibiades 4'? Obviously not, and hardly less obviously the right
reading here is Κῦρος β' (cf. κύρβας), i.e. the second of the Cyrus
dialogues. This had the alternative title Περὶ βασιλείας, and Cicero's
interest in it at a time when he was trying to compose a Συμβουλευ-
τικόν to Caesar (12. 40. 2) needs no further commentary.

12. 39. 2   Read as follows:

de tabellariis facerem quod suades, si essent ullae necessariae
litterae, ut erant olim, cum tamen brevioribus diebus cotidie
respondebant tempori tabellarii. *at* erat aliquid, Silius,
Drusus, alia quaedam. nunc, nisi Otho exstitisset, quod
scriberemus non erat; ⟨*et id*⟩ ipsum dilatum est.

at *scripsi, puncto praeposito*: et Ω   et id *addidi,* id *Cratander*

Cicero says that he would act on Atticus' suggestion (whatever it was) to secure a more regular exchange of letters, if there was any 'necessary' correspondence, as there used to be when the carriers did keep to time despite the shorter daylight. *But* in those days there were matters of business afoot, now there are none, except the Otho affair; *and* that has been put off.

13. 17. 1   nunc eadem illa, quid Brutus cogitet, aut, si aliquid egit, ecquid a Caesare.

et quid RΔ: corr. Lambinus

ecquid a Caesare means 'quid [or rather 'ecquid'] afferatur de eius adventu' (Manutius), not '"whether there is any intimation from Caesar" as to how he regards the action of Brutus' (TP). That is obvious from other passages: 13. 9. 2 . . . *cum Caesar venerit; de cuius adventu eam opinionem Dolabella habet quam tu coniecturam faciebas ex litteris Messallae*, 13. 16. 2 *Brutus ecquid agit et quando? de Caesare quid auditur?*, 13. 21 a. 3 *de Caesaris adventu scripsit ad me Balbus, non ante Kal. Sext.* Something has fallen out: *quid Brutus cogitet, aut, si aliquid egit,* ⟨*quid egerit*⟩, *ecquid a Caesare. et quid* could be kept, but the choice is free since *ecquid* is regularly so corrupted in these MSS.

13. 19. 3   sed quia ⟨*scribis*⟩ et desiderari a Varrone et magni illum aestimare, *eos* confeci et absolvi nescio quam bene *et sqq.*

So the vulgate. But *scripseras* not *scribis* (ed. Romana) gives the appropriate tense. *eos* (sc. *libros*) is difficult since the books (the *Academica*) have not been mentioned. Reid wished to delete it. If Cicero had meant 'those books which you know of' he would surely have written *illos*. I think he wrote *hos*.

13. 23. 3   quare da te in sermonem et *perseca* et confice et ita cum Polla loquere ut te cum illo Scaeva loqui putes.

perseca et *bms*: perseca *RMd*   et ita cum Polla *OR*: excita compella Δ

Polla is unknown, but *excita, compella* is wholly inappropriate. Cicero is not urging Atticus to be energetic, but to be conciliatory in dealing with Caesarians who cannot be expected to waive their legal rights. As for *perseca*, its continued presence in texts (without obelus) is a scandal, not to be excused by the uselessness of proposed substitutes: *persece, persta, perfice*. The right word is *praesta*, 'give [or 'promise'] them their money'. For this financial use of *praestare* cf. for example 10. 11. 2 *ut non cupiat tibi praestare*, 14. 16. 4 *puto . . . praestaturum eum.*

13. 32. 1   Postumium autem, cuius statuam in Isthmo meminisse te dicis *sciebam* fuisse. is autem est qui ⟨cos.⟩ cum ⟨L.⟩ Lucullo fuit; quem tu mihi addidisti sane ad illum σύλλογον personam idoneam.

> cos. *et* L. *add. Wesenberg*   sciebam *PΔ*: annis sciebam *Zᵝ*

Cicero was contemplating a πολιτικὸς σύλλογος *more Dicaearchi* (13. 30. 2), the scene to be laid at Corinth in 146. The Commission of Ten sent out to assist Mummius could provide some suitably distinguished πρόσωπα. The previous day he had asked Atticus to ascertain their names (ibid.). He himself knew or thought he knew of three, including 'the consular Albinus'. Atticus' reply was now to hand, and it evidently brought to Cicero's attention the name of A. Postumius Albinus, who held the consulship along with L. Licinius Lucullus in 151.

Since Cicero clearly did *not* know that this man was at Corinth until Atticus told him, *nesciebam* (Muretus) must be accepted. But that is not enough. For he did know, and had so written the day before, that a consular Postumius Albinus was among the Ten. He was presumably thinking of Sp. Postumius Albinus Magnus, consul in 148, the only other living consular Albinus. In accepting Atticus' information about Aulus he was bound to mention the praenomen; for whether both Aulus and Spurius were among the Ten, or (more likely) only Aulus, the salient point was that Cicero had known of a consular Postumius at Corinth, but had not known of Aulus Postumius. Read therefore ⟨*Aulum ne*⟩*sciebam fuisse*—'I did not know that Postumius, whose statue you said you remember in the Isthmus, was Aulus Postumius'. This explains *annis sciebam* which Bosius read in *Z*: it came from *anesciebam*.

This Aulus was a *doctus homo* (*Acad.* 2. 137), notorious for his interest in Greek culture (see Münzer, *RE, Postumius* no. 31); hence Cicero's acclaim.

13. 37. 1 has alteras hodie litteras. de Xenonis nomine et de
Epiroticis xxxx nihil potest fieri nec commodius nec aptius
quam ut scribis. *id* erat locutus mecum eodem modo Balbus
minor. nihil novi sane, nisi Hirtium cum Quinto acerrime pro
me litigasse *et sqq.*

So editors; but in the MSS. *minor* is followed by a second
mecum, which they delete—very properly if the result were satisfactory, but it is not. The younger Balbus is not likely to have been
mixed up in these business affairs of Cicero's, while he is a natural
source for the information about Quintus (cf. 11. 12. 1). Gronovius
was on the right track: *is erat locutus mecum eodem modo. Balbus
minor nihil novi sane* et sqq. But the second *mecum* should stand:
Balbus minor mecum; nihil novi sane et sqq. Cf. 14. 10. 3 *ibi eum
Balbus mane postridie, eodemque die mecum in Cumano; illum here-
ditatem aditurum* (so punctuate).

15. 1. 4 See p. 73. 'τὸ ἐκ τούτου *Z¹*': so Lambinus in his first
edition, but in that of 1573 τὸ ἐκ τού ου and τὸ ἐκ τοῦ οὖ in that of
1584. The sequence suggests that the later reading may be a typo-
graphical error, and his note 'unde facile facere licet τὸ ἐκ τοῦ
αὐτοῦ' points the same way. On the other hand τὸ ἐκ του ου is in
Bosius' 'anecdota' (*Zᵝ*).